D0016144

**ON BEING**

**JOHN McENROE**

# On Being John McEnroe

*Tim Adams*

crown publishers new york

The author and publishers make grateful acknowledgment to the following for permission to reproduce previously published material: *Serious* by John McEnroe (Little, Brown), courtesy of Time Warner Books UK; *The Diaries of Kenneth Tynan* by Kenneth Tynan (Bloomsbury), courtesy of Bloomsbury Publishing; and "The Subaltern's Love Song" by John Betjeman, from *Collected Poems* (John Murray), courtesy of John Murray (Publishers) Ltd.

Published by Crown Publishers, New York, New York.
Member of the Crown Publishing Group,
a division of Random House, Inc.
www.crownpublishing.com

Originally published in Great Britain by Yellow Jersey Press, London.

CROWN is a trademark and the Crown colophon is a registered trademark of Random House, Inc.

Printed in the United States of America

DESIGN BY BARBARA STURMAN

*Library of Congress Cataloging-in-Publication Data*
Adams, Tim.
    On being John McEnroe / Tim Adams.—1st American ed.
  1. McEnroe, John, 1959–   2. Tennis players—United States—
Biography.   I. Title.
    GV994.M26A33   2005
    796.342'092—dc22                              2004013369
ISBN 1-4000-8147-5   3225 0556 ⁴⁄05

10 9 8 7 6 5 4 3 2 1

First American Edition

To Lisa

I've seen him slay Goliath with a pea-shooter, seen him win tournaments just by being there. By being John McEnroe.

—PETER FLEMING, doubles partner

ON BEING

JOHN McENROE

# Perfect Day

In the summer of 1983, I queued up for most of a drizzly night in south London to watch John McEnroe play the unseeded American Bill Scanlon in the last sixteen at Wimbledon. To pass the time in the queue I'd brought a couple of books to read. One of them was J. D. Salinger's *Raise High the Roof Beam, Carpenters*. I'd not long before read *The Catcher in the Rye*, and had developed a carefully worked out theory (I seem to remember) that McEnroe was, in fact, a latter-day Holden Caulfield, unable and unwilling to grow up, full of complicated genius and unresolved conflict, constantly railing against the phonies—dozing linesmen, tournament organisers with walkie-talkies—in authority. I'd brought the novella along therefore, I imagine, in a dubious kind of private homage—my only defence is that I was seventeen—or at least in the pretentious belief that it would make an appropriate preface to the next day's match.

In any case, when I was reading it in the grey dawn halfway down Somerset Road, a particular passage stuck in my head. Salinger was struggling to describe the idea of perfection in one of his characters' lives, and the closest he could get to it was a tennis match. Perfection was, he suggested, a feeling like "someone you love coming up onto the porch, grinning after three hard sets of victorious tennis, to ask you if you saw the last shot he made."

It undoubtedly seermed to me then, and it still just about seems to me now, that this was the kind of feeling that John McEnroe was always restless for, and sometimes able to communicate in his game: a kind of instinctive euphoria. He'd found it a few times in his matches against Bjorn Borg, but at the age of twenty-four, after his great rival had retired prematurely, it already looked like he was struggling to summon that kind of heightened sense. As a result he was looking more angry and disconsolate than ever.

Certainly that was the case on that heavily clouded afternoon against the prosaic Scanlon. McEnroe won somewhat disdainfully in straight sets, using all the angles, berating himself and the officials, scratching his head, tugging at the shoulders of his shirt, having a great deal of trouble at changeovers with the lacing of his shoes, searching all the time for something like the appropriate sense of occasion. He had never, of course, looked entirely comfortable on a tennis court, constantly vigilant as he was for the one thing that was ruining it all for him that day—a spectator with a cough, a television microphone—but all through that year's tournament, which he won by beating the starstruck Kiwi Chris Lewis in a hopelessly one-sided final, he played as if something was absent from his life.

I had a sense then, watching him desperately try to find some kind of self-respect, that the thing which was missing, the thing that had been taken away from him, and from the rest of us, was the real shot at perfection or fulfilment which his games against Borg had offered.

He had needed something in his rival to make himself feel whole.

Nearly twenty years later, when I asked him about this during an interview in Chicago, he agreed with the interpretation. "In 1981 when I beat Borg in the Wimbledon finals and then beat him at the US Open, suddenly, out of nowhere, he stopped playing the major events," he said. "To me it was devastating, if that's the word. . . . I certainly got very empty after that because it had been so very exciting up to that point. Of course, there were other great challenges—Ivan Lendl and Jimmy Connors—but it was so natural with Borg. Our personalities were so different, the way we played was so different, nothing ever needed to be said."

Great tennis players, like great chess players or great boxers, cannot exist in isolation: they require a rivalry, an equal, to allow them to discover what they might be capable of. When Andre Agassi returned to the game after his self-imposed break "at the buffet table" in his midtwenties, Pete Sampras, his nemesis, sent him a heartfelt note expressing relief that he was back. McEnroe tried, every time he met Borg, to persuade him to return to tennis, but he never really got even an explanation for the Swede's retirement.

When I asked him how he thought their matches would have gone had Borg not retired, he thought for a moment before suggesting that he believed they would both have got better and better as players and, probably, as people, "and that might have been something to see. . . . As it was I found myself lost a bit. I pulled it together, and played probably my greatest tennis in 1984 [the year he dismantled Connors in the Wimbledon final, making only three unforced errors], but even at the end of that year I felt not at all happy. There was this void," he said, "and I always felt it was up to me in a sense to manufacture my own intensity thereafter."

# Self 1 and Self 2

## t w o

John McEnroe had first seen Bjorn Borg play when he was working as a ball boy at the US Open at Forest Hills in 1971. The Swede had already, at fifteen, begun to make a name for himself and collect a hormonal following of schoolgirl fans. Though only three years his senior, to McEnroe—and no doubt to the schoolgirls—Borg looked very much like a grown-up, a state to which McEnroe himself subsequently struggled to aspire. (Like Richie in Wes Anderson's film *The Royal Tenenbaums*, McEnroe was in part entranced by the brevity of Borg's kit: "the Fila outfit, the tight shirts and short shorts . . . I loved that stuff!"). He later had, alongside those of Rod Laver and Farrah Fawcett, a poster of Borg on his bedroom wall.

By the time they got to play each other, Borg was already established as the world's number one. He had won three Wimbledons and three French Opens; he was living as a tax exile in Monte Carlo; and he had long silenced the adolescent screams of most of his following with the almost pathological reserve and concentration he displayed when playing: there seemed no way to get to him.

McEnroe, though, was determined to break through that mental armoury. He and Borg first met on court, appropriately enough, in Stockholm in 1978, at Borg's home tournament, in front of the Swedish royal family, who had come to observe the smooth progress of their champion. McEnroe, never a great respecter of form or expectation, beat Borg, and his legend, 6–3, 6–4. It was this victory more than anything—more than his spectacular debut Wimbledon of 1977, when he had reached the semifinal as an eighteen-year-old qualifier and taken a set off Jimmy Connors—that convinced him he could achieve something in the game: "If I could beat Borg," he said, later, "then I knew I could beat all the others."

For Borg—who won only 7 points on McEnroe's serve in that match—that initial meeting held a particular significance, too. It was the first time he had ever been beaten on the tour by someone younger than himself—the first hint, perhaps, of the knowledge that eventually comes to all prodigies: that he, too, would grow old.

To understand anything about McEnroe, it seems first necessary to examine his relationship with Borg. Well before their monumental struggle in the Wimbledon final of 1980, McEnroe had resolved both to establish the Swede as his greatest rival and to eclipse him. Most gifted young tennis players hope to get into the top ten or the top five, but McEnroe always believed he could be number one. With this in mind, he first worked extremely hard to be accepted as a peer of Borg's, both on and off the court. By the time of their Wimbledon meeting in 1980, he was getting closer to his hero. He had beaten Borg twice more, but the Swede was up 4–3 in matches. They had, too, been partying together along with their mutual friend and master of revels Vitas Gerulaitis.

Borg could see McEnroe coming. In a pictorial autobiography published the week before Wimbledon, Borg examined the contenders for his number one position in 1980: "Jimmy Connors has been my most intense rival for six years," he wrote. "But at the moment, John McEnroe has the game to give both Jimmy and me sleepless nights. His style is flexible while Jimmy's is rigid . . . but the fury of a McEnroe/Borg rivalry has not yet had a chance to boil over. It's still simmering."

At the same time, McEnroe conceded that "sure, we act differently on court. Once in New Orleans when I went berserk over a call he gently waved his palms up and down to calm me. When we play, the match is always going to be interesting, because of our contrasting styles, with me trying to rush the net and him staying in the backcourt. Sometimes when he and Connors play it's dull because they both stay in backcourt until someone misses. The most satisfying place for me to beat Bjorn? The French Championships in Paris on clay over five sets."

Like Muhammad Ali and George Foreman, or Boris Spassky and Bobby Fischer, both McEnroe and Borg seemed immediately to see in the other qualities and philosophies that they lacked in themselves, both as players and people. Perhaps unlike those other rivals, though, they each seemed to love the other for his difference. For Borg, McEnroe possessed spontaneity and instinct and was a source of constant surprise. "It sounds strange," he noted, "but he has more touch than Nastase. He is a master of the unexpected. I can never anticipate his shots."

For McEnroe, Borg had patience and calm and something like grace. Most of all, he loved the "cleanness" of Borg as an opponent, compared to his own psychological mess. "Borg accepted me," McEnroe suggests, as if that is all he ever wanted. "There was a level of respect there that I never really reached with anyone else. It was as if he were saying to me, look, we are hitting a tennis ball over the net and this is a pretty damn good way to make a living. And here I was going crazy and thinking he was about to call me an ass. It was beautiful in that way."

Anyone who has played tennis at any level knows that on court is one of the few places where, generally speaking, you are allowed to talk to yourself, even if it is only to say "C'mmmmmmmooonnnnn!!!" (like Lleyton Hewitt), or "C'mon!" (like Tim Henman). At the time that

McEnroe's game was forming, sports psychology was be-coming big business. Few players took a therapist on the road with them, as many do now, but analysis was in the culture, and it was only a matter of time before it be-came applied to tennis, which, in its balance between extreme action and contemplative inaction, and its re-lentless examination of the individual, is perhaps the most mentally fraught of sports.

Many coaches sought to employ the techniques of therapy to their players' advantage, but few were as suc-cessful as W. Timothy Gallwey, who, at the age of fifteen, had missed a heartbreakingly easy volley for match point in the National Junior Tennis Championships in America and always wondered why. In 1976, the year of Borg's first Wimbledon triumph, Gallwey published a little book called *The Inner Game of Tennis*, which was pitched, in the spirit of the time, as being somewhere between *Zen and the Art of Motorcycle Maintenance* and *How to Win Friends and Influence People*. In it he observed that when most people played the game they routinely divided themselves in their heads and, typi-cally, one half of their self railed at the other half, the half that was serving double faults and fluffing volleys.

"Imagine that instead of being two parts of the same person," Gallwey wrote, "Self 1 and Self 2 are two separate persons. How would you characterise their relationship after witnessing the following conversation between them? The player on court is trying to make a stroke improvement. 'Okay, dammit, keep your stupid wrist firm,' he orders. Then as ball after ball comes over the net, Self 1 reminds Self 2, 'Keep it firm. Keep it firm. *Keep it firm!*' Monotonous? Think how Self 2 must feel! It seems as though Self 1 doesn't think Self 2 hears well, or has a short memory, or is stupid. The truth is, of course, that Self 2, which includes the unconscious mind and nervous system, hears everything, never forgets anything, and is anything but stupid."

To achieve any kind of success, in tennis, or in life, Gallwey went on to suggest, Self 1, the conscious, nagging, neurotic mind, had to be prepared to get off court. If tennis were taken as a paradigm for life in general, and in particular that kind of modern life which threw pace and spin at you in equal measure, then "the most indispensable tool is the ability to remain calm in the midst of rapid and unsettling changes. The person who will best survive in the present age is the one Kipling described as he who can keep his head while all about are losing theirs. . . ."

In writing this, Gallwey might have been describing Borg, who was almost unique among tennis players in managing, or at least appearing to manage, to take the emotional, self-doubting side of his mind entirely out of his game. In 1980 Borg was insisting, also along with Kipling (whose poem "If" greeted players in the Wimbledon locker room) that "once a match is over, it's over. I don't carry either the pain or the glory with me."

Gallwey would not, however, have known where to begin with McEnroe. The psychologist argued, employing a new phrase, that " 'freaking out' is a general term used for an upset mind. For example, it describes what happens in the mind of many tennis players just after they have hit a shallow lob, or while preparing to serve on match point with the memory of past faults rushing through their minds. Freaking out is [also] what stockbrokers do when the market begins to plunge; or what some parents do when their child has not returned from a date on time. . . . When action is born in worry and self-doubt, it is usually inappropriate and often too late to be effective."

If Borg sought to remove the fretting of his conscious mind from play, to let habit and faith in his physical strength and skill take over, McEnroe seemed unable and often unwilling to quiet the voices in his head for even a moment. Every shot he played, even his soft-handed instinctive volleying, appeared, to some degree, to have been born out of a titanic internal struggle with "worry and self-doubt." His face and body language constantly betrayed the fact that he wanted to question the integrity of every ball he went for, every move he took, and every decision he or anyone else made on court.

All players, even Borg, might have thought momentarily about their shot selection and the state of their world before they hit the ball, but only McEnroe seemed always to be thinking about it as he played the ball. When I watched him then—and still when I see him play now—I was convinced that the ball seemed always to spend fractionally longer in contact with his racket than it did with the racket of his opponent. He rarely hit at the ball; rather he pushed it or placed it or angled it, using the pace it already carried. He talks about how, the first time he ever picked up a racket, he could "feel" the ball through the strings, as if he were touching it (a recent BBC advert for Wimbledon appositely had him playing faultlessly with his hands) and he seemed to use that sensation to apply all of his complex mental energy to each shot.

McEnroe remembers being obsessed, as a boy, by the way in which the mind might be constantly kept in play during a point, and this moment-by-moment concentration has never left him: "I loved to take my racket back for a hard forehand or backhand, and then, at the last millisecond, feather the ball over the net," he said. As a child, he hated routine practice. When the coach of his junior squad, the legendary Australian disciplinarian Harry Hopman, came around to organise drills, he would often hide. Even when he got to the top of the game he did not put many hours in on the practice court, still fewer in the gym; he used his doubles matches, increasingly considered a distraction by the other top players, to refine his instincts, and to keep fit.

The contrast between Borg and McEnroe—between, if you like, Selves 1 and 2—was most apparent in their preparations for Wimbledon in 1980. Borg stayed at the Holiday Inn in Hampstead, north London, where he always stayed. Each night he set the air conditioner to

12 degrees Celcius (53.6 degrees Fahrenheit) and slept naked with no blankets for ten hours. His pulse rate on waking was never above fifty beats a minute. He maintained his body weight for the duration of the tournament at exactly 73 kilos (160.6 pounds); anything else, he believed, altered his balance and took the edge off his reflexes.

Two days before the tournament began he had a two-hour massage with his coach, the giant former Swedish Davis Cup captain Lennart Bergelin. As Borg's then fiancée, the Romanian tennis player Mariana Simionescu, recalled, "It is more a torture session in which the athlete Bergelin breaks loose. Lennart's strong fingers don't spare a single square inch of Bjorn's body, but Bjorn takes it all in silence as if it were an initiation rite." The night before his opening game, Bergelin and Borg, as they always did, took his fifty highly strung Donnay rackets and, for a couple of hours, tested their tension by gently hitting them together and listening to the sound they made. Each racket was then laid on the floor according to its relative musical pitch, an arrangement not disturbed for a fortnight, save to remove, in order, the six rackets he would use in each match.

On the morning of a match Simionescu would pack his kit in a special sequence, the shirts, the headband, the socks, all with their own place in his bag, and he would watch her doing it while he "anointed" his feet with moisturiser, ever vigilant against blisters. When they drove from Hampstead to Wimbledon, a journey of perhaps an hour, Bergelin would, regardless of traffic, always take exactly the same route, so as not to present Borg with any small off-court surprise. At the All England Club he always asked for the same chair he had sat on at changeovers in the previous victorious years and for two towels, never more or less, to be placed beside him. He was in thrall to superstition. His parents were permitted to attend only in alternate, even-numbered years, since he had lost in 1975 and won in 1976.

On court he had, similarly, single-mindedly attempted to remove all that was unnecessary from his play, including anything that might look like self-consciousness. His shots, though viciously powerful, were presented with the minimum of flourish. He played always, on any surface, to his own strengths, which were his remarkable speed and stamina, and his ability to out-concentrate any player in the world. His strokes, typically the whipped topspin forehand and two-fisted backhand, were so ingrained as to be beyond thought. As a nine-year-old he had played by himself, seven hours a day, hitting the ball against his garage wall, always conducting an imaginary Davis Cup tie, Sweden vs America: if he hit for more than ten consecutive times Sweden won the point (they remained undefeated for years). By the age of twelve, he was playing nine hours, seven days a week.

Through this early drilling Borg had forced himself to focus always on what was occurring rather than what had occurred or what was about to occur. If he missed a shot in a match Borg never, as every other player did on occasion, went through the motions of replaying it as he swapped sides. This was, he said, just "vanity . . . as if you would like to prove you could do it correctly, and circumstances independent of your will forced you to commit the error." He tried to keep the circumstances that were independent of his will to a minimum, but, highly unusually for such a controlling personality, he had cultivated in himself an ability to accept that there were some things he could not control. The last time Borg had questioned a line call was in a Davis Cup practice nine years earlier, when Bergelin had, in response, pushed him over a bench, thrown a racket at his head, and dropped him from the team for two days.

Every aspect of Borg's game and life was, in other words, designed to allow little or no dialogue between Self 1 and Self 2. When he played, there was no division in his mind. "Freaking out" was never an option.

McEnroe's mental preparation for Wimbledon fell some way short of Borg's monastic ritual: often it consisted of listening to Joan Jett and the Blackhearts on his headset; his diet always included McDonald's and pretzels. Because of this, more than anyone in his sport, or maybe any other, McEnroe appeared to me on occasion to capture the idea that the game was just that, a game, something you played at, and were forced instinctively to make up as you went along, whatever the psychological consequences of this effort.

When he first played McEnroe, the 1975 Wimbledon champion Arthur Ashe felt that "whereas against Borg you feel like you're being hit with a sledgehammer, this guy is a stiletto. [McEnroe] just slices people up. . . . It's slice here, nick there, cut over here. Pretty soon you've got blood all over you, even though the wounds aren't deep. Soon after that you've bled to death." Each time McEnroe went on court, each time he addressed the ball, he behaved as if he was starting from scratch, looking at it for the first time. You could begin to argue, as some sportswriters did, that his matches were like action paintings, or jazz solos, or the creative efforts of a writer faced always with a blank page.

This was nowhere more apparent than in his service, which began with him side on to the court and bent double, stooping to drag ball and racket out of nowhere. McEnroe originally started serving that way at the US Open in 1978 because of pain in his lower back, and found that it allowed him to get more disguise, and to throw himself farther into the court to prepare for his volley. More than that, though, the action seemed to give him time to think, or at least to gather his wild and whirling thoughts, and to deliver the ball as if it were a concentrated act of will. (As Clive James observed, watching Wimbledon in 1980: "You have to realise that McEnroe is serving around the corner of an imaginary building and that his wind-up must perforce be extra careful. He has a sniper's caution.") The effect generated was not unlike that produced by those Chinese table-tennis players who appeared at about the same time and who threw the ball way up towards the ceiling lights, waiting an eternity for it to come down before delivering it with devilish pace and spin. Each time McEnroe slowly wound himself up at the service line it looked, in some sense, as though it was his last big shot, a final throw of the dice. And then, of course, he would do it again.

In talking of the effect his kind of neurotic engagement had on people who watched him play, McEnroe believed that he touched the reality of people's lives far more viscerally than Borg ever did. "The way I acted on a tennis court was more the way people acted in life," he suggested. "It's an extremely frustrating game, and difficult to do right. We all have situations every day that make us want to yell. What Borg did seemed unbelievably hard to do. It was weird. Every now and then I'd go on the practice court and say, hey, today I'm going to act like Bjorn, I'm not going to say anything. And it would maybe last like five shots. It didn't seem right."

Thus, when Borg and McEnroe walked slowly out on

to the Centre Court at a quarter to two on July 5, 1980, the crowd should certainly have been prepared for more than a simple tennis match. What they were about to see was at least as much a confrontation between two highly developed states of mind: a struggle between extreme consciousness and an absolutely studied containment of consciousness.

This fact was betrayed as soon as the two finalists emerged from the locker room and set foot on court. Borg's stride, as he made his way to his familiar chair, was perfectly measured, his face entirely impassive. McEnroe's gait, meanwhile, his head rolling a little from side to side, his hand rubbing at the nape of his neck, was reminiscent of that *New Yorker* cartoon in which a man is walking along the street, looking down at the pavement and at his own feet coming and going. "The right foot has disappeared," he is saying to himself as he walks. "With any luck the left foot will be appearing any moment now."

When he reached his chair, McEnroe chucked his pile of rackets down and stretched out—as Mariana Simionescu, watching from the family gallery, observed—

"as if he were lying on a deck chair on Miami Beach." Her beloved Borg, meanwhile, sat down carefully "like a concert pianist trying to find the best angle for his knees"; he cradled his rackets lightly, and quietly peeled the cover from one.

And then both men prepared themselves to play.

# "Oh, I say"

#### three

For the English, tennis is not so much a sport as a fortnight. The show courts of the All England Lawn Tennis and Croquet Club are used for two weeks per year, and if you were to land in the country for the first time during those fourteen days, you would have the impression that tennis was a vivid national obsession. Tennis stories make the front page and the back page of the daily papers. Middle-aged newspaper editors apparently become mesmerised by fleeting glimpses of the undergarments of teenage hopefuls in the ladies' draw. There is much anguished optimism, and doomy resignation, about the fragile resolve of that early summer's great British hope (Virginia Wade, John Lloyd, Jo Durie, Tim Henman . . . ). And then, hope fast extinguished, for the remaining fifty weeks of the year, save when Britain is losing a zonal Davis Cup match to Paraguay or Turkey: nothing. None of the other Grand Slam events is properly televised, and the weekly grind of tennis players, and their undergarments, in places like Tashkent and Conakry is confined to the "In Brief" sections of the sports pages.

Because John McEnroe mostly came to London only for those two weeks, however, he was initially a little like the monarch who believed that all the world smelled of new paint. He found at Wimbledon a degree of self-absorption that almost matched his own. As he readied himself to take on the world, he realised that his primary battleground would have to be SW19. If he needed Borg to discover who he was and what his game could achieve, then he seemed also instinctively to understand that he required the unwritten niceties of the English middle classes to test that self against.

It was not just the venerable history of the tournament, or the way in which the fast grass of Centre Court suited his sliced service—it was more the fact that he could always rely on Wimbledon to react to him. Unlike Borg, who remained entirely impassive in the face of McEnroe's psychological frailties, Wimbledon would invariably respond with a mixture of purple outrage and curious nannying, and therefore always let him know that he and his anguish were, as the therapists liked to say, real.

This became apparent to McEnroe in his first match on Number One court, as an eighteen-year-old, against an Australian called Chris Dent. Dropping a service game, struggling with his rhythm, cursing his fates, McEnroe put his racket under his foot at one lost point, and bent it until it nearly broke. He then heard a sound that he had not heard before in the gloomy green hush of the court, the sound of booing. It was something like music to his ears. He bent the racket some more, and the booing got louder. He felt suddenly at home. Up until that moment the only noises from the packed crowd had been muted clapping at miraculous volleys and some nervous coughing and the rustling of grease-proof sandwich papers at changeovers. He kicked the racket from the middle of the court slowly all the way to his chair, and the booing got louder still.

As the satirist Craig Brown once suggested, in a parody of McEnroe's worldview, there was a part of him that would like to have believed that the British are all "driven round by liveried servants, eating strawberries and cream with their monocles in the back of horse-drawn carriages. And you know what?" wrote Brown, in the McEnroe idiom. *"It gets in my face."* If McEnroe had confined his understanding of Britain—or more precisely of England—to the hierarchies at Wimbledon in the late 1970s, however, he could almost have been forgiven such a misapprehension.

The All England Club was run, with some precision, by Air Chief Marshal Sir Brian Burnett. When he was about McEnroe's age, Burnett had held the world's long-distance flight record of 7,158 miles, which he achieved, in 1934, by flying from Egypt to Australia. He had commanded the 51st bomber squadron during the war and subsequently become aide-de-camp to the Queen, who was herself patron of the club. Burnett's committee included two dukes and a lord as well as his eventual successor, "Buzzer" Hadingham, the chairman of Slazenger, and former commander of 302 antitank battery in the Italian campaign, in which he had been awarded the Military Cross for valour at Salerno.

It might be fair to say that these men were of the view that tennis, however enjoyable and beneficial for the soul, was not the most important thing in the world, and that tennis players, accordingly, should know their place. They also held that the Corinthian spirit of the game, as it was originally patented by their fellow officer Major Walter Clopton Wingfield in 1874, was to be preserved at all costs. Wimbledon had come of age as part of the Season, which included the Henley Regatta and Ascot. It was, traditionally, as much a playground for the entrants in *Who's Who* as those in the singles draw, and the Victorian distinctions between Gentlemen and Players remained somewhere near its heart.

It had been only after much soul-searching that Burnett's predecessors had admitted professionals to play at the club in 1968. You might say that the committee still distrusted money, or at least the effect it had on games. Wimbledon was the one arena in competitive sport, or in fact in just about any area of life, that had stoutly resisted the march of advertising: there were—

and are—no billboards on Centre Court (apart from the players). The only commercial endorsement allowed was for Robinson's Barley Water, a brand that earned its place at courtside because it had been invented there, in 1934, when a couple of players got thirsty and a spectator added some barley to the lemonade. Some within the All England Club had entertained fears when the tournament became open that something of its spirit would be diluted. With the coarse aggression of Connors, the intimidating gamesmanship of Nastase, and the scowling torments of McEnroe, many of their worst fears were being realised.

The rules of the club, written and unwritten, were quietly enforced by the tournament umpires, many of whom, perhaps because of Burnett's influence, conceivably for their eyesight, were also Royal Air Force officers. They were, for the most part, men not used to insubordination from mouthy teenagers with distinctly nonregulation haircuts. Moreover, wing-commanders, for example one George Grimes, an umpire who docked a point from McEnroe in the belief that the American had described him as a "disgrace to mankind," were not at all prepared to argue the toss in public about their decisions. (McEnroe's defence in this instance was that he had been talking to himself, but, since he made the comment while pointing towards the umpire, a man whose judgement and authority and manhood he had been questioning under his breath for much of the previous hour, the defence was shaky, even if vehemently maintained. "I wasn't talking to *you*, umpire. *Do you hear me? What did I say? Please tell me!*")

In the British fashion, these kinds of confrontations tended to be cast for the public in military terms, international sport being routinely employed as a metaphor for our place in the world. Ian Wooldridge, then sportswriter of the year, bizarrely suggested that McEnroe, who was born in Germany (albeit on an American air force base, where his father was serving) had all "the charm of a Hitler Jugend führer, and the sort of arrogance you might expect from a double VC, except that double VCs tend to be rather shy." (Rather shy, he might have added, and probably on the committee of the All England Club.)

Participants in the tournament had always been expected to come to Wimbledon full of the kind of sentiments expressed by Gordon Forbes, a South African player of the 1950s and 1960s, who published in 1977, the Queen's Silver Jubilee and the tournament's centenary year, a charming memoir of his time on the tour called *A Handful of Summers*. Forbes, who had arrived for his first Wimbledon by ship from South Africa, wrote how he found himself "suddenly in the sun, [with] the soft old Centre Court, lying waiting, all green, waiting, for two o'clock . . ." before confessing how his emotions had got in the way of his progress to the second round. "I was moved to tears, as I took court for my opening match, so that I dropped my first serving game due to burning eyes, and finally lost the match . . . I watched Drobny win that year . . . saw him out-think Kenny Rosewall. Marvellously deft tennis, all poise and balance. At match point deafening silence fell. Then Rosewall's backhand return snapped up against the tape and the Wimbledon people leapt to their feet. They had grown to love 'Old Drob,' as they called him, and wanted him to win, and he stood there, all smiles."

McEnroe may have had tears in his eyes at certain stages of matches on Centre Court, but they weren't for the ghosts of Wimbledon. The players' traditional subordination to the ideals of the club included their being required to bow to royal cousins who lived on pepper-corn rents in London palaces. McEnroe was never going to be happy in the role of court entertainer. "It's unusual for me to see, for example," he said, with some under-statement, of his first tournament, "the way when roy-alty come in you have to bow. Here you are, supposedly the person that's out there for people to see, but you have to bow, and you're not even from that country."

These sentiments were particularly pointed in 1977, with the Queen attending the tournament. McEnroe was not alone in his New World indifference to the fact. Jimmy Connors was among the first players to be booed on to court at Wimbledon after missing the Centenary Parade of Champions because he was practising for his opening game on an outside court with Nastase. He had, apparently, not realised the ceremonial importance of the occasion. "Jim's here to play tennis," a friend explained, without quite acknowledging that Jim had thereby com-mitted almost as much of a treasonous snub to the established order of things as Johnny Rotten, who had lately been cruising down the Thames to announce by megaphone that Her Majesty was a moron.

The sense of deference extended, in McEnroe's

eyes, to the club's facilities. He was "appalled initially at the way the organisers of Wimbledon treated lesser players," though he reacted to this with typical New York pragmatism, conceding he had "better get to the top . . . so I could be treated well, too."

These divides had long been enshrined. When Fred Perry, England's last singles champion, won the first of his three Wimbledons in 1934, he overheard a committee member of the All England Club apologise to the Australian Jack Crawford, the runner-up: "This was one day when the best man didn't win." Although Perry was a homegrown champion, the committee man was embarrassed that somebody of his background, the son of a Labour MP from Stockport, should have been victorious on Wimbledon's patrician lawns. "Instead of Fred J. Perry the champ, I felt like Fred J. Muggs the Chimp," Perry recalled. The committee's disquiet extended to the crowd, because, Perry suggested, "they had never really seen an Englishman who didn't like to lose. . . . I was confident and I was arrogant, because in one-to-one confrontations like boxing and tennis you have to be." Perry, in later life, believed McEnroe to be "a genius who can start to make his stroke, then hold back if he has to. . . . He is the one player in the game who knows exactly where his racket is at all times, and exactly what his options are." He also thought that the American "was asking for a whacking," and that, had they played, McEnroe would have had the Perry racket "right over his head."

Whereas for Perry, McEnroe's worst crime was that he sought to intimidate his opponents; for Sir Brian Burnett it was that after he had argued with an umpire, he did not seem to acknowledge he had done anything wrong. In part, at least, this had to do with the clash between cultures. McEnroe's insistent question to Wimbledon's officialdom was, How serious do you really want this to be? And, though they would never quite admit it to him, their answer was, Well, not quite as serious as you, sonny.

Virginia Woolf once characterised this kind of difference between English and American attitudes to sport in a discussion of the fiction of Ring Lardner, whose stories often featured the internal dramas of sportsmen, prefiguring those of Hemingway, or Salinger: "Mr Lardner's interest in games has solved one of the most difficult problems of the American writer," Woolf observed. "It has given him a clue, a centre, a meeting place for the diverse activities of people whom no tradition controls. Games give him what society gave his English brother. . . . In America there was baseball instead of society."

This distinction just about held true in 1980. As John Self, the hero of Martin Amis's novel *Money*, remarked before stepping out onto a $200-an-hour Manhattan tennis court—in a borrowed pair of checked Bermuda shorts and ill-fitting tennis shoes—to pitch his dodgy forehand and nonexistent backhand against the grooved strokes of his American business associate: "I should have realised that when English people say they can play tennis they don't mean what Americans mean when they say they can play tennis."

When the English talked about playing tennis, there was still just a hint about it of John Betjeman's:

> . . . *strenuous singles we played after tea,*
> *We in the tournament—you against me!*
>
> *Love-thirty, love-forty, oh! weakness of joy,*
> *The speed of a swallow, the grace of a boy,*
> *With carefullest carelessness, gaily you won,*
> *I am weak from your loveliness, Joan Hunter Dunn.*

As with most things in Britain—the constitution, say, or the law—Wimbledon, its "carefullest carelessness," was based on a series of unwritten rules and codes, with their basis in precedent and tradition, the enforcement of which rested on an insider's knowledge of how things should be done. One effect of McEnroe's "hobbledehoy antics," Peter Wilson of the *Mirror* pointed out, meant that "you look for the rule book as often as you look at the court."

In response to this argument, McEnroe was fond of saying, simply, that he knew his rights. He took an American pride in the fact that he employed, in his early years at least, the rhetoric of the judiciary when arguing with umpires—"Answer the question!"—conducting his case for a bad line call in "a lawyerly way." (His father, looking on, was a partner in the firm Paul, Weiss, Rifkind, Wharton & Garrison in New York City; his brother Mark was at law school continuing that family tradition; and there was much about McEnroe himself that suggested he was a frustrated hanging judge.)

He knew, at least, that he was at liberty to request to have a linesman changed, for example, or call for the referee, even if the person who emerged when he made that request was Fred Hoyles, a farmer from Lincoln-shire, or Alan Mills, who, with his walkie-talkie ever to hand, always seemed to me to be doing a passable imitation of the man who wasn't there. The point, however, that McEnroe had failed to grasp was that though in England you were, of course, *allowed* to call for the referee, that did not mean you were actually supposed, under any circumstances, *to call for the referee*. It was as if Tom Paine had come back to life, woken up with a hangover, picked up a racket, donned a crimson headband, and ruined a lazy Sunday-afternoon picnic with his pedantic obsessions about things like truth and justice.

One of the fixtures at Wimbledon in those days, along with Dr. Barnardo's ball boys and the Duchess of Kent, was Teddy Tinling, formerly a good county player, who in the English way had lacked any semblance of a killer instinct on court (and whose game had often been hampered, he suggested, by his playing "his backhand with his forehand grip, and his forehand with his backhand grip"). Tinling had instead made a name for himself as a tennis-dress designer. Most significantly, he had pandered to middle England's underwear fetishists by becoming knickers-supplier to the stars: he had put

Maria Bueno into frills, lavished proprietary attention on the gusset of Gussie Moran, and reportedly designed a pair of pants for a forward-thinking Australian player that had her telephone number embroidered on the backside (it remained there until her boyfriend noticed as she crouched to receive serve). Tinling summed up McEnroe's crimes with characteristic aplomb when he observed: "In Britain it has always been accepted in polite society that certain things are best left unsaid. He is a divisive force in our little world because he forces people to take positions they'd rather not take."

That McEnroe was quite so divisive, however, was perhaps a result not only of what he said, but of the historical moment in which he was saying it. In 1980, the "little world" of which Tinling spoke, the All England Club that was British society, found itself under threat from all sides. In the Jubilee year, David Gray, the late *Guardian* tennis correspondent, had argued that "We British may be monsters of indiscipline at football [soccer] matches, but at Wimbledon, by Gum, we are models of decorum. . . . At the end of June we make our pilgrimages to the All England, carrying our sandwiches, our Thermos flasks, our books of reference, and hoping that we glimpse Mark Cox threading his way home through the crowds." If not Orwellian myths of warm beer and spinsters on bikes, at least Wimbledon gave us iced Pimm's and Air Chief Marshals.

Outside Wimbledon, though, things were changing very fast. In the summer of 1980 Margaret Thatcher had already spent a year loosening the ties that bound us. Unemployment in Britain had risen since the previous Wimbledon by 850,000, more than in any other year since 1930. Led by government, there was a general cynicism about much that stood for tradition. Faith in institutions began to plummet to all-time lows. Every Saturday afternoon those "monsters of indiscipline," soccer fans, many of whom, in a curious inversion, favoured Fred Perry's laurel-wreath tennis shirts as their brand of choice, created ad hoc fight clubs in shopping centres and railway stations up and down the land.

The gentle England of Thermos flasks and "Oh, I say" was, in other words, beginning to look like something of a museum piece, even to those who still held the faith (to many of us it had always looked like that). Mrs. Thatcher had been elected on the basis that she would import American ideals of winner-takes-all economics and, to some establishment eyes, McEnroe looked a lot like the living, spitting embodiment of that new free-market individual. His behaviour signalled the end of deference in the most deferential of sporting arenas (he thought—along with much of the rest of society, it seemed—that "we'd had enough of manners and curtsying to rich people who didn't pay any taxes"). Most of all, he demonstrated on court the kind of naked self-obsession that seemed to characterise the decade that followed—while he was playing there was no such thing as society.

The uneasy nature of this new Britain he found himself in was apparent in his relationship with the press. On the one hand McEnroe's on-court behaviour prompted predictable harrumphing editorials—which affected outrage at the fact that "he challenges authority, a disturbingly fashionable trait among youths AND their parents" —as well as reports which admonished him, for example when he won the title at Queens Club in 1980, for "having kept his left hand in his pocket while greeting the Vicomtesse de Spoelberch, who was presenting the trophy." Conversely, the tabloids, led by Rupert Murdoch's *Sun*, which were themselves beginning to wage a personal war on the establishment, seized on McEnroe's attitude and exploited it for all it was worth.

McEnroe was first called Superbrat in the *Daily Express* after he complained about a pigeon fluttering in the hall at Wembley in November 1978, and he subsequently was made both a poster boy for the decline in public behaviour in Britain—the emergent hooligan culture—and one of the first tabloid sacrifices to the ever-growing public appetite for celebrity gossip.

He was unused to and unable to deal with the intrusion. Just as he disliked the fact that he was expected to play a certain role to the crowd, he had no wish to be so easily pigeonholed by the media. He attempted to defend his rights, such as they were, to privacy. When the young Alastair Campbell of the *Mirror* (later architect of New Labour's PR machine and the Prime Minister's spin doctor in chief) fronted him up to ask if he accepted that millions of youngsters copied him, McEnroe reportedly "snarled" and said, pointedly, "You should take a look in the *Mirror* and see who is screwing up the kids." Before adding, somewhat presciently, "The power you have is sad."

When Campbell asked him if he had any regrets

about his behaviour, McEnroe responded (prophetically, for a generation of parliamentary correspondents) that "My only regret is that I have to deal with people like you."

On other occasions he suggested that "maybe it doesn't matter, ultimately, if some [paparazzo] takes a photograph of you. I guess if you can get to the stage where it doesn't matter, then it doesn't matter. But I never got to that stage. *It always mattered to me.*"

Most players responded to the gentle questioning of the mandatory postmatch press conference with a kind of bored diffidence, and mouthed the usual clichés about focus or the lack thereof. McEnroe, unable or unwilling ever to switch off in this sense, could never go through the motions. The great *Guardian* sportswriter Frank Keating attempted to interview McEnroe in 1980. Before he had a chance to ask a question, McEnroe, typically, had set the ball rolling: "I suppose," he started, "it will be the usual dumb stuff—'Why don't I ever smile?' and 'Why am I rude to officials?' And 'Why can't I be more British?' Well, let me say I don't smile when I'm concentrating on work—well, do you go around with a grin on your face when you're reading up some concentrated research?—and, as for being rude to linesmen, well I honestly say I've only ever queried what I genuinely know is a bad call. I just think my eyesight at 20 is better than some old man's of 70, however much he might love tennis. Anything else?"

For Keating, playing the role of ingénue when faced with the sportsman whom he believed to be perhaps the most charismatic since Muhammad Ali, there was not really anything else. "He looks at you," he wrote, "this pouting, freckled Just William who has been dressed up as Hiawatha in a Sunday school play, and you say: 'No, John. Thank you, John. That just about covers it, John'—and you curse yourself for not daring to ask why he's so fixated about his plimsolls and the laces therein."

What the newspapers, or the Wimbledon commentators, were slow to pick up on, however, was that much of Britain, far from being shocked by the behaviour of McEnroe, actually enjoyed and identified with it. He voiced some of the nation's own frustration and anger at the way our institutions were run—often amateurishly—by the same old boys' club of peers and grandees.

It was, then, perhaps no surprise that this kind of

sentiment would be published in the *Guardian* letters page: "How we sporting English love it. A rebel being mauled by a system, which he bucks because he has a keener eye and redder blood." But when the *Telegraph*, the voice of the Establishment, ran an editorial about McEnroe's behaviour, it subsequently had to run nearly a page of responses in his support. "I feel very sad when I contemplate what is happening to young McEnroe," confided one reader. "He is a very rare, indeed a unique talent, amounting to genius, which I fear is to be crushed out of existence by a small-minded, rigid tennis establishment. What is his crime? He smashed a ball into some netting behind the court. . . . As for the crowd, their savage baiting of a defenceless youth makes me feel quite sick. No wonder he is goaded into petulance. Should we not treasure a unique talent and try to solve the psychological problem that goes with it, rather than simply destroy it?" Another reader, from the stockbroker belt of Surrey, suggested simply, "I find all his matches on television vastly entertaining, which is more than I can say for some of his predecessors, who used to make me drop off in front of the box."

Despite these kinds of reactions, when the 1980

Wimbledon final came around there remained an assumption that the nation would be rooting in overwhelming majority for the steely sportsmanship of Borg. One newspaper was astonished to find, however, that, in a straw poll, about half its readers actually wanted Superbrat to prevent the Swede from winning his fifth title. Deference, it seemed, playing the game, was becoming dull. Borg, with his reserve and never-say-die determination, looked a lot like how England once thought it wanted to be; McEnroe, restless, self-obsessed, had begun to look increasingly like how it was.

# Sudden Death

#### four

Every tennis fan remembers where they were on Saturday, July 5, 1980. Nelson Mandela had managed to persuade his guards on Robben Island to provide a radio so he could listen to the World Service commentary. Andy Warhol had got up early in his mother's old house on East 66th Street, Manhattan, to catch the game on the networks. Sachin Tendulkar, in Bombay, destined to be the world's greatest cricketer, was dressed, aged seven, in a tennis kit and scarlet headband in homage to his hero, McEnroe. And I was struggling with the aerial on an old portable TV in a caravan, in a field overlooking the grey sea on the coast of west Wales, where the same rain—and hail—that had interrupted that year's tournament had also served to dampen an already angsty teenage family holiday. For me, the tension of the match was heightened by the fact that I had hardly been outside for a week, except in a mackintosh. And also because, on crucial points, the television picture had a tendency to begin revolving at a furious rate, causing McEnroe, crouched interminably to serve, to begin frantically chasing several versions of his crouched self up and down the screen.

He started, I remember, too easily. Though it was McEnroe who had had the tougher semifinal, against Connors the day before, it was Borg who looked stiff and even a little slow. The Swede was chopping short-arm returns into the net, jabbing at forehands, unable to find any feel for the ball. McEnroe was dominating with serve, punching and feathering volleys by turns. Many tennis matches (including almost all the ones I ever played in) simply carry on this way. One player (invariably this was me) is unable to summon any semblance of rhythm or grace, and simply throws away the match in a series of unforced errors.

In the first set, at least, that looked like it might just be the case for Borg in 1980. As a result, walking back to his chair having established his lead, McEnroe seemed particularly ill at ease: just as he hated to lose, so he apparently took no pleasure at all in winning too comfortably. He scratched his head, picked at his socks, bit his lip. "I get a feeling from time to time," he would say, speaking for many of us, "when it feels like things are going too well, that something bad has to happen." Something, on this occasion, was very horribly wrong: he was 6–1 up against the four-time champion.

Up in the stands, Borg was being watched by Mariana Simionescu, who was keeping notes on her feelings during the match, in preparation for a book that was to be her wedding present to him. The previous night, at the Holiday Inn, she'd had a dream: "I am in Greece and Bjorn is far out to sea, and he comes back with a lot of fish. We cook the fish on the beach. Our little house is far above and you have to climb exactly 134 steps to get to it, and we eat there, on the sand, with wooden spoons, and Bjorn has never been a tennis player." She is not quite sure what to make of this dream, but somehow it does not seem like a good omen. Her horoscope has told her: "If possible, don't leave your house today."

When the players came out for the second set Borg still looked awkward, but seemed untroubled by the way he was playing. He made no effort to shake life into his arms, or to stretch his legs. He played, that is, as he always played, looking for the next shot and the next point. The crowd, which sounded equally split between the two players, was muted, though, as if wondering whether the King of Wimbledon was going to give up his crown with hardly a whisper. McEnroe had been saying before the match that he thought the "Wimbledon crowd just wants Borg to win for ever," but that this time, "McEnroe was in his way." It seemed odd for him to talk about himself in the third person, as if he were not sure he had a real say in the matter.

Apart from a few die-hard partisans, the allegiance of a tennis crowd, and in particular a British tennis crowd, tends to shift depending on the state of the match. If it is a close struggle, or a final, then it will support the player who is just behind, in order to prolong

the game into something memorable (so that the spectators get their money's worth). This is not how the crowds
feel in soccer, say, when there is a finite length to the
match, whatever the score. But a one-sided tennis match
is hardly a match at all. For this reason, having been rooting for McEnroe, I recall now willing Borg to come back,
to make something more of it.

Replaying the match again, it looks as if McEnroe
wants to feel his way through the second set, to get it
over with quietly. Recognising that Borg is not on top
of his game, he also starts to play just a little within himself, not hitting the lines but just inside. But still he is
well on top. Borg gets nowhere near his serve and clings
on desperately to hold his own. Then, at five games all,
Borg locates his timing for just a couple of points. Once
he starts hitting the ball he starts moving better, and
suddenly he has served a love game and has broken
McEnroe for the first time, to take the set.

McEnroe looks, at this point, like he has been am-
bushed and humiliated. He squats down on his haunches,
juts out his lower lip; tears seem a possibility. A man in
the crowd with a pink silk open-necked shirt and a cigar
clamped between his teeth stands up to cheer the

Swede. Mariana Simionescu in the stands is angry at herself for having ever doubted that her betrothed, King Borg, would let her down.

At one set all, now it is McEnroe's turn to look stiff and out of sorts. The American player Gene Meyer remarked how, the first time he played McEnroe, on any given point his opponent "never seemed quite ready, whether serving or receiving." And he does not seem ready now, twitching a little, taking an age to wind up his serve. He overhits a couple of volleys, sets up Borg at the net twice. And he is 3–0 down in the third set, having dominated the whole match. At changeover he takes off both his shoes and peers inside, as if looking for what has gone wrong. He then bites furious lengths of sticking plaster off a roll and makes little loops of them, which he lines up along his thigh, before attending angrily to his shoelaces. A couple of weeks earlier, in Queens, his opponent, Sandy Meyer, Gene's brother, had offered to tie up the laces for him, believing he was using it as a tactic to disrupt his serve. McEnroe had replied as Woody Allen might have done: "I'm just a very fidgety person . . . I don't know why . . . I always like my laces to be very tight, especially for crucial points." Before he goes out to serve he leaves a little pile of sticking plaster loops beside his chair.

Borg does not worry about anything, apart from his rackets, the strings of which he taps to listen for a reassuring tone. Other than this, he occasionally blows lightly on his fingers. At changeovers he looks up without expression at Simionescu and Bergelin. He and his wife-to-be have a code during matches. Sometimes he feels he wants her to leave, believes she is getting in the way of things, and he indicates this by making a curt slicing motion with his hand, down by the pocket of his shorts—the kind of behaviour which perhaps, in retrospect, did not augur particularly well for their marriage. On this occasion, she is pleased to see, he is happy for her to stay, and she makes mental notes as he wins the third set. "The crowd now seems to breathe in a special way," she senses, "as if everyone is adjusting to his pulse."

The most memorable tennis matches are those which invent their own rhythm. In the early sets you begin to notice little patterns within points, themes and metres, which are then returned to and tested under the greatest pressure at or near the death. We remember the 1980 final primarily for the tiebreak. But there were epic moments before that drama which seemed to enable it to be possible. There were the three break points Borg saved at 4–4 in the second set, the loss of any of which would almost certainly have put him down two sets to love. And then there was the twenty-point game he served at 4–2 in the third set, with McEnroe always an inch or two away from breaking him back and restoring parity. On both occasions it was Borg who had held his nerve and prevailed, as he always prevailed. These exchanges were stored in the memory of both the players and the audience, and as the tension developed, both we and they, subconsciously perhaps, expected them to be repeated.

In the fourth set both players play at a pace and with a confidence that had not previously been apparent. McEnroe goes through his full repertoire of shots—stop volleys and drop volleys, angled passes and lobs—but Borg is chasing down nearly everything now and passing McEnroe at the net on both sides. On other occasions, in other matches, McEnroe could become overwhelmed by the sense that "I'm out there on the line, by myself, fighting to the death in front of people who are eating cheese sandwiches, checking their watches, chatting about the stock market." Now, though, no one is eating their sandwiches, and he has what he has always required: the crowd's full attention.

Even so, just an hour after he appeared to have the match and the title within sight, he is now facing defeat. Matches involving Borg often seemed to work out like that. Vitas Gerulaitis, Borg's closest friend, who had never beaten him in sixteen attempts, once said: "Every time I play Borg I come out with some thirty new ideas which should get me victory. And each time Bjorn breaks each one of the thirty to pieces, like a clay-pigeon shooter." The Swede looks in that mood now, his eyes apparently getting closer together, zeroing in, and eventually, at 40–15 and 5–4 down, McEnroe faces two match points.

Before he settled himself to receive the first of these serves, you could see—even, I remember, on my intermittently revolving TV screen—McEnroe searching his armoury at this moment, wondering what he might throw at Borg. It looks a bit like the wonderful frame or two in the film *When We Were Kings* when the camera lingers on the face of Muhammad Ali, who, having exhausted what he thought was everything against George Fore-man, quietly determines simply to let himself be hit for a few rounds to tire out his opponent. In something like this spirit McEnroe looks down at the ground and swipes at a piece of loose dirt at the service line, wondering what manner of man he is playing. And then he con-ducts two entirely thoughtful rallies, different from what has gone before, pushing the ball around the court, let-ting Borg feel the pressure, and ending with nerveless passing shots. He finishes off the game with two extra-ordinary backhands, not so much struck as guided over the net. And having been dead, he is now alive.

The very greatest competitors are, it seems, always motivated not by the glory of success but by the abject fear of the pain that attends defeat. Boris Becker once described this sensation very clearly. "When you are a young man, you are looking for your own identity, and winning is a way of expressing yourself. When I lost, I wanted to die. And because I thought in victory I became somebody, in defeat, it followed, I was nobody." In the showers at Wimbledon, after he had successfully retained his singles title at the age of eighteen, Becker bleakly shouted through to his coach that he did not feel as strongly about having won the championship as he had a couple of years before when an ankle ligament injury had forced him to withdraw. "Winning," noted his coach, "never lifts him as high as losing drags him down." It was the same with McEnroe, too, who talked about being "diminished" in defeat, of not being the man he hoped he was.

In a tiebreak, as in a penalty shoot-out in soccer, the burden of this kind of little death is only ever a shot or two away. This fact is reflected in the emotion of the crowd: its empathy is not at all with the person who will win the match but entirely with the person who will lose it.

The tiebreak had been introduced in 1971 and McEnroe had grown up with it. His father once told a story about a tiebreak he had watched his son play at the Pepsi Junior tournament in Forest Hills, when he was sixteen. "He had six or eight match points; some were net cord balls, and luck was against him. When it was over he was on court with his face in his hands and a towel over his head. I don't normally do it, but I went over to him on court, and said: 'Don't worry about it, son; it's not so bad.' He didn't want to talk to me, though—he was too upset. I was upset, too. I mean, it was a *horrible thing* to witness."

Günther Bosch, Becker's coach, suggested that "in a tiebreak there are no benevolent spirits you can pray to; it's not a poker game or voodoo. A player must be peaceful and calm inside. He must open the door and go quietly into the room." But the Wimbledon final did not allow that kind of calm, at least not to McEnroe. If the match was Borg's to win, it was McEnroe's to lose. "Somehow," he later remembered feeling, "maybe because I'd saved those match points earlier, I could sense that people who didn't want me to win the match, wanted me to win the tiebreaker. They just didn't want this match to end. And the match itself did not seem to want to end."

The idea of a tiebreak is a simple one: kill or be killed. On this occasion, though, I remember thinking how the two players seemed to be anxious to explore a third option: that of a death indefinitely postponed. As the points stacked up, the commentators' talk turned from "the long walk" and "staring down the barrel" to desperate hopes of closure: "Well, *surely* now . . ."; "And *finally* the champion serves for the match, for the *sixth time* . . ."

At 11–11, we were told, there was "nothing left now to happen." But there was plenty more to happen. Once they are into the teens, the points seem to go faster, and the possibility of ending seems oddly further off. There is a net cord on match point; a service called out is over-ruled before McEnroe has a chance to explode; and then he misses two easy volleys. Watching the close-up of him now, at 14–14, he seems to be wondering if he should give up the game for good.

Simionescu, meanwhile, smoking with her cigarette cupped in her hand below the ledge in front of her, so that Borg won't notice, starts producing metaphors at the rate of one a point. Having thought initially that the tiebreak was "like the drum beating that heralds the tumbril carrying the convicts sentenced to death . . . like a dawn in the Middle Ages when all the balconies are booked because no one wants to miss the moment of the beheading," she now believes "that the stadium is a boat at the mercy of a giant wave, bobbing on the crest only to be sucked into the abyss the next moment." At

15–15, "The audience is still; even the heads have stopped turning from right to left, from left to right. These fortunate few are watching, in fact, two men walking on a tightrope between two tall buildings, who go steadily ahead to meet at the middle, where one will have to fall." At 16–16 she feels she is witnessing a moon landing; at 17–16 they are all in an aquarium. And then, 18–16, she watches Borg fall from his tightrope at the twentieth floor; the scoreboard wipes away everything and comes back up with two simple numbers, 2–2, and the players return to their seats.

After the tiebreak, having lost seven match points, Borg quietly checks his rackets again. McEnroe begins violently chewing something; he sends a ball boy on an errand that the ball boy clearly does not understand, but which he is far too scared to question. Their brief exchange ends with McEnroe telling him to just "go; go now."

And then there follows a moment which must rank among the greatest in sport. It is the moment when Borg walks out to serve once more, two sets all, one set to play, as if nothing had happened. "I thought Borg would be physically deflated after losing the tiebreaker," McEnroe said. "But whatever he had inside him was beyond anything I could imagine." McEnroe had forgotten his fatigue during the tiebreaker, but now he was beginning to remember it. "At one point I started getting cramp in my foot. Then my knee hurt. But I pushed myself anyway. I felt I did my best. It was, like . . . like I was playing from within."

Borg, though, had gotten to that place first. He won the final set 8–6, winning all of his last five service games to love. Afterwards, when he was sitting in his chair, zipping up his rackets, the camera caught him for the first time in what looked like reflection. He tried an odd half-smile and muttered something to himself, a single word, in Swedish. The word meant "unbelievable."

He had not been dethroned, but for the first time Borg admitted in the postmatch interview to something in his head that he had not allowed the public or his opponents to see before at Wimbledon: doubt. When asked if he was unsure of the eventual winner at certain stages during the match, he said, "Yes, of course." It felt like a moment to reach for the book of quotations. Richard Evans, writing in *Tennis Week*, observed: "Thank

God for McEnroe for otherwise Borg would indeed 'be-stride this narrow world and hold the palm alone.' "

Immediately after the interview Borg phoned his parents in Sweden. They were asleep at nine o'clock, and he apologised for having woken them up. He then did not speak for a couple of hours, not to Bergelin, not to his fiancée, Simionescu. Later he went to a reception at the Clermont Hotel, where Petula Clark and Shirley Bassey sang to him "Happy Wimbledon to You." Someone produced a cake. Two weeks after that, he and Simionescu were married.

# Men and Boys

## five

Initially, the BBC muffled courtside microphones when John McEnroe was playing at Wimbledon, much in the way that the Victorians used to cover piano legs. Therefore many of his early hands-on-hip streams of consciousness to umpires and linesmen were difficult to decipher, even, as I discovered, if you were two feet from the screen with the TV volume turned up to possibly dangerous levels.

Occasionally, though, a sentence would get past the broadcaster's sound police—"You are the pits of the world"; "You two sit there like bumps on a log" — and the nation would be left to ponder the exact meaning behind its baroque flourish. At some point the BBC, itself groping for new boundaries of public decorum, must have found that the sound track was generating at least as much interest as the passing shots and half-volleys and so, in the interests of, well, voyeurism, they tended to let it run.

Even when we were allowed to hear only fragments of McEnroe's rage, though, there was something more than a little cathartic about it. "To be honest," he said, perhaps summing up a more general feeling, "I think everyone these days is easily irritated. I just show it more obviously than most people. Most people aren't in touch with themselves, or true to themselves." Though we'd never admit it, he was probably right.

In his decade-defining book *The Culture of Narcissism*, appropriately first published in Britain in the summer of 1980, the American historian Christopher Lasch identified this dislocation as the chief characteristic of our age. He argued that "people [today] have erected so many psychological barriers against strong emotion . . . that they can no longer remember what it feels like to be inundated by desire . . . they seethe with an inner anger for which a dense, overpopulated, bureaucratic society can derive few legitimate outlets."

McEnroe playing tennis personified exactly that kind of "inner anger" as well as its release in strong emotion. He was, in Lasch's terms, a model of contemporary "Psychological Man" who was defined as being "plagued by anxiety, vague discontents, a sense of inner emptiness, [and struggling for] peace of mind under conditions that increasingly militated against it." That struggle was dramatised for the viewing public every time McEnroe stepped onto court.

Arthur Ashe, the Wimbledon champion of 1975 and the only black man to win the title, confessed how a part of him responded to this rage. In the 1980s Ashe had acted as McEnroe's Davis Cup captain, and experienced some of his more extreme on-court meltdowns in pursuit of the record five titles that he helped America to win (in particular a stand-up fight with the Argentinian José Luis Clerc, who had lispingly questioned his manhood). A man of few and always carefully chosen words, Ashe was a perfect gentleman on court, and most observers assumed that he despaired of McEnroe and was ashamed, on occasion, to have him in his team. However, in his memoir, *Days of Grace*, published not long before his death from AIDS, Ashe refuted these suggestions. "Far from seeing John as an alien," he wrote, "I think I may have known him, probably without being aware of my feelings, as a reflection of an intimate part of myself. The sense of McEnroe embodying feelings I could only repress, or as a kind of darker angel to my own tightly restrained spirit, may explain why I always hesitated to interfere with his rages. . . . Now I wonder whether I had not always been aware, at some level, that John was expressing my own rage, my own anger, for me, as I could never express it."

Ashe's bottled-up feelings were undoubtedly shared by a good proportion of Britain's tennis-watching public—never the most emotive of groups—many of whom perhaps found a similar kind of relief in McEnroe's dramatic self-exposure. As the 1980s progressed and McEnroe's rage seemed to darken, the television coverage of tennis, and of Wimbledon in particular, began to pander, consciously or not, to all of these vicarious possibilities.

Tennis always looked like it was made for television. It was the right shape, for a start: one of the few sports where all of the playing area could happily be contained on screen, and also one which kept its cast of characters, of "personalities," to a minimum.

The Wimbledon fortnight, in this sense, became the nation's first annual reality TV show, twenty years ahead of its time, catering to the growing appetite for armchair psychology and a collective colonisation of the interior lives of celebrities. It was almost as if the tournament had been custom-built for this purpose: there was an artificial arena and a group of intense, photogenic young men and women, scantily clad and placed under extreme and unusual pressure on a daily basis. Their faces were constantly scrutinised by a battery of cameras; the court was wired to catch their every muttered soliloquy (a process helped by the fact that tennis was the only aggressive sport where quiet was politely demanded of spectators). This controlled environment was policed by officious men and women in suits, and deconstructed for the viewer by a whispering gang of experts.

McEnroe, particularly after 1980, found himself the star turn in this arena, and the attention he received extended well beyond the confines of the court, as print journalists began to exploit the process of manufacturing and manipulating myths around TV celebrities, which were made to fit simple black-and-white narratives. (At around this time, journalists at the *Sun*, who led this trend, took to calling their ongoing celebrity soap operas, in which McEnroe became a reluctant villain, "fairytales.")

Richard Schickel, the author of *Intimate Strangers: The Culture of Celebrity in America,* observed how, by 1985, the coverage of Wimbledon had come to look a lot like the future. "As an American who frequently visits England," he wrote, "I have come to admire the discreet role television plays in your life — only four channels of it, broadcasting in a generally sober, often dull, fashion. Setting aside your peculiar relationship with the royal family — the only 'celebrities' with whom you maintain an ongoing, highly subjective American-style relationship — Wimbledon represents, as far as I can tell, your *only* major breach of decorum. . . . As a result of the tournament's exposure on TV, it has attracted millions who can barely distinguish a lob from a passing shot and who can understand what is going on only in terms of star personalities portrayed in crude terms — what amounts to a form of popular fiction. . . . If you can imagine 100 Wimbledons proceeding without stop all year long—one for politics, one for each of the arts, one for social issues, one for crime—all of them trivialised for TV's convenience, then you have a fair sense of how American public life now proceeds."

Some players began to look for ways to limit their role in this drama. A few took to placing towels over their heads during changeovers to avoid the gaze of cameras and crowd, like defendants on their way to court. Others, like Borg and later Sampras, managed to make their faces a mask that revealed little of what was going on inside—only to be criticised as "dull" for refusing to give the public access to the thing it increasingly desired: their emotions. McEnroe was unable to employ any of these strategies. Rarely had a face evinced so much anguish, and never had its every tic and grimace been broadcast instantaneously across the globe.

There had always been an existential quality about tennis, in the demands it made of the individual. Even the South African Gordon Forbes, whose memoir was something of an exemplar of old-style decorum, recalled how once, in a far-off hotel room, he noted in his diary that "All tennis matches are lonely," before detailing the moods in which he won and lost. The former involved, he believed, "Loneliness, plus Courage, Patience, Optimism, Concentration, a Calm Stomach and a Quiet Deep Fury." The latter included "Loneliness, plus Fear, a Hollow Stomach, Impatience, Pessimism, Petulance, and a Bitter Fury at Yourself." Whereas once these states of mind, in the heightened atmosphere of Centre Court, had been a private kind of communion between the player and the few thousand spectators, now they were magnified in close-up and bounced off satellites to all corners of the world. They became, to many, the point of the contest. When McEnroe "misbehaved," betrayed his "loneliness" or his "quiet deep fury," never before, in Britain at least, had such displays of real-time emotion—which later became the staple of the talk shows that now fill the daytime schedules—been so widely disseminated.

McEnroe's extremes of moral outrage affected people in different ways. Jack Higgs, an American professor of English, argued in an essay in 1985 that "McEnroe is—or rather has been—the only highly and genuinely indignant person I know of or have even read about. Could more of us summon forth such righteous indignation and direct it at social issues," he went on, "we would have Utopia within the year."

Others saw in McEnroe a misunderstood hero. Tom Hulce, who played Mozart in Peter Schaffer's Oscar-winning *Amadeus*, created his very contemporary infantile genius with McEnroe in mind: "I needed a model," Hulce explained. "McEnroe resembles Mozart by his attitude. John is young. Talented. Shining. But he cannot be kept silent. He refuses to take account of the rules. People compare themselves to him and try to control him because of his lack of control. That's exactly what happened to Mozart."

Sir Ian McKellen, rehearsing *Coriolanus* for the Royal Shakespeare Company, looked to McEnroe, too, as an exemplar for the righteous anger of the rebel leader: "It's not that . . . with Coriolanus I started walking around like McEnroe or trying to look like him or speak like him," he explained. "It's just a reassurance that there can be someone at the top of his game—like Coriolanus, who's the great, great warrior but who has something in his spirit which despises the praise as much as the criticism that he might get from the crowd. It's looking for the humanity in that way."

A little like Coriolanus, McEnroe was all too acutely aware of his place in the goldfish bowl and part of him came to despise it. Trapped and taped and forced into a role by the media, he began symbolically to take issue with the means of that reproduction, the hardware of the global village: he swiped his racket at humming microphones near the umpire's chair, kicked at courtside TV monitors, and became anxious about the electronic seeing eyes that were introduced to assist line judges and bring to an end the arguments that he had mostly initiated. "I don't want to sound paranoid," he said, of the "Cyclops," which monitored the service line on Centre Court, "but that machine knows who I am." The greatest regret in his tennis career was that he lost his best chance of the French Open, in 1984 when two sets up in the final against Ivan Lendl, because he became infuriated with the crackle of a cameraman's headphones. It was as if he could suddenly hear the white noise of the world bearing in on him. McEnroe picked up the headset and instructed the world to "shut the fuck up," but his concentration, and the match, were lost.

The great contradiction for McEnroe, in this sense, was that—bizarrely—given his apparently unchecked megalomania, he seemed to desire above all not to have to make a spectacle of himself. To the crowd at Queens Club in 1981, he yelled: "I'm so disgusting you shouldn't watch. *Everybody* leave!" He became addicted to public attention but hated both himself for needing it and the public for wanting a piece of him. Boris Becker, a character of similar complexity, later complained how in his early days he felt extremely exposed on the show courts, as if in thrall to the appetite of the crowd: "I know they are silently looking me up and down," he said. "I always react the same embarrassed way. I bend down and tie my shoelaces although it's unnecessary. They don't want to see you—they want to *have* you."

Unlike Connors, say—miming sex acts with his massed ranks of fans at the US Open—or Nastase, who became a master of crowd manipulation, with easy jokes and crude slapstick, McEnroe could never bring himself to give the audience what it desired of him. Instead he seemed more comfortable when alienating his public. Sometimes this took the form of direct action: at Boston's august Longwood Club in 1979 he spat at a woman spectator who clapped at a double fault. (Later, when faced with this allegation, McEnroe adopted an admirably Clinton-esque defence: "I spat in front of her," he said. "I didn't *get* her.") More often, it was conveyed in his refusal to smile, still less to laugh, on court. He explained this by saying that he believed this kind of posturing demeaned not only himself but also the occasion: "To put humour into a big tennis match felt like being a phoney, I guess. It would mean I wasn't a true competitor, a real athlete. It smacked of professional wrestling."

Despite this, McEnroe sometimes made halfhearted efforts to win over the English: each Wimbledon after 1980 was prefaced by protestations, elaborated in the tabloids, that he was a reformed character and that he needed the crowd to love him. But he only had to step out on court for those fantasies to be rejected and the front-page headlines to be rewritten—GO HOME, SUPERBRAT. "I was never able to let the crowd know that I needed some help," he admitted in his autobiography. In a world now requiring not character but caricatures in fairy tales, he desired above all to be his own man.

The playwright Alan Bennett, who would sometimes have you believe he was the last defender of that lost England of Thermos flasks and car blankets, is not, by his own admission, the keenest student of tennis. Still, he found himself musing on some of these ideas during one early morning cycle ride through Camden Town in the summer of 1981. He became so involved in this kind of thinking, he confided to his diary, that his lips would form the words and passersby would stare, not out of recognition, but because he looked like a lunatic.

The substance of his internal monologue was how, "now that Wimbledon is all about money, behaving badly is exactly what is required, certainly of McEnroe, and all the claptrap about decency and fair play is just the English at their usual game of trying to have it both ways.

"Wimbledon is now a spectacle," he muttered to himself, "just as a wrestling match, say, is a spectacle, and a spectacle needs a hero and a villain. Not because McEnroe is particularly badly behaved but because the Wimbledon authorities have sold out to television and this kind of drama is just what viewers enjoy."

If Bennett was correct in his judgement, then, as with all the best long-running television dramas, this one increasingly became centred on the family.

Tennis is unique in that it is the only sport in which we come to recognise and "know" the parents of the protagonists. Television cameras do not pan on to David Beckham's Mum and Dad after every free kick he takes at Old Trafford; they never cut to Herr and Frau Schumacher when their sons are on the podium at Monte Carlo; they stop coyly short of examining the expression of Mrs. Lewis when young Lennox is getting thumped in Las Vegas. But between almost every game at most tennis tournaments, and on Centre Court at Wimbledon in particular, the viewers are allowed, and required, to interpret the emotions on the faces of the players' mothers and fathers, in close-up.

The tensions read into these relationships come to establish little narratives of their own. As Tim Henman, tournament by tournament, grows to look more like his father, stoic and unblinking in his blue club blazer, we are invited to wonder if son, like father, would benefit from being a little less buttoned up. When Pete Sampras finally let us in on his family after his record-breaking Wimbledon final in the millennium year, it was presented as if, after all this time, he had finally given in and got in touch with something like his feelings.

This kind of family drama is all the more compelling for the viewer because relationships between tennis stars and their parents, it is fair to say, even by the standards of the time, are often more than usually complex. The trend was begun in earnest in matches involving Jimmy Connors, who read for inspiration from his late grandmother's tearstained letter during changeovers in his defeat by Arthur Ashe in 1975, while his mother, Gloria, looked on from the stands. Gloria had already set the mould for a certain type of extravagantly pushy tennis parent. A nationally ranked player herself, she had coached Connors from a very early age, basing his game on aggression: "My teaching theory has always been to punch the ball," she said. "Jimmy was brought up to *belt* the ball, not just paddle it. I emphasised power, not finesse." At Connors's matches, Gloria tended to reiterate those virtues in unambiguous terms: "Kick him in the slats, Jimmy!" she would yell.

As more and more money came in to tennis, the pushier—and more destructive—tennis parents became. In the women's game, where girls were often chaperoned in their early years on tour, there were casualties everywhere you looked. The American Mary Pierce had a restraining order put on her abusive father. Peter Graf, father of Steffi, was imprisoned in Germany for his handling of her financial affairs. Martina Hingis, then the world number one, walked out on the French Open final, and her mother and coach, in tears, claiming she could not stand the maternal pressure any longer. Jelena Dokic's father quickly succeeded in alienating the entire tennis establishment on two continents as his daughter shifted nationality on his whims.

The most extraordinary drama, even by these standards, was, however, that conceived by Richard Williams, who planned the tennis careers of Venus and Serena before they were born (having first, the legend has it, sabotaged his wife's contraception). He then put his girls through his homemade tennis education on public courts, and saw his apparently wild predictions that they would become the world's number one and two players fulfilled almost immediately when they turned professional. When Venus won her first tournament, Williams sat in the family gallery holding up a placard reading: "I told you so." His pride in this incredible achievement was matched only by his subsequent delight in winding up the white male tennis establishment in general, and its journalists in particular, inviting and parodying their intrusiveness. (For a while, his telephone carried the following answering machine message: "Hi, I'm Richard Williams. There are those who want to ask me what I think of intermarriage. Anyone that's marrying outside of this race that's black should be hung by their necks until sundown. Please leave a message after the tone. . . .")

In the men's game the standard for parental obsession was set by Mike Agassi, who at seventeen had represented his native Iran as a boxer in the Olympics, and then, having emigrated to America, found himself work as a waiter and a stringer of tennis rackets in the casino hotels of Las Vegas. Most of his considerable energies, however, he directed towards the tennis coaching of his four children. The three eldest—Rita, Philip, and Tammee—were all schooled daily using service machines that their father had adapted to fire balls at a higher than normal velocity on a court he had laid himself in their backyard. By the time little Andre was born in 1970, Mike Agassi had his methods honed: he hung a tennis ball above the baby's crib to develop his hand-eye coordination, taped a racket to his hand as soon as he could walk, and when he was two had him serving overarm on a full-sized court. At the age of five Andre was praying for rain in the Nevada desert so he would not have to practise.

A couple of years ago I interviewed Agassi and he still spoke with some complicated sadness of this childhood. "You don't know anything else when you start playing before you can remember," he said. "I did not know life away from it. It's kind of like a tortured soul, you know. You have a choice but you don't have a choice. There are times when you look forward to quitting and times when you don't imagine ever possibly doing anything different." Agassi banned his father from sitting in the family seats, unable to handle the world eavesdropping on their peculiar relationship.

Set against these dysfunctional Freudian sagas that held a mirror up to our broken-home times, McEnroe's relationship with his parents appeared extraordinarily well balanced. They had ensured that he enjoyed a far more varied upbringing than most of his peers in the game. His father, John senior, the son of a first-generation Irish immigrant to New York, had put himself through law school in evening classes. He had risen to become a partner in a prestigious firm, and could afford to send his children to the city's best schools.

McEnroe went to Buckley Country Day School (one model for Holden Caulfield's Pencey Prep) and then Trinity High, founded in 1709 by the charter of Queen Anne, and the oldest school in New York. He excelled at Latin under an English-born classics master, and combined top grades in most subjects with a mastery of sports: he was quarterback for the football team, guard for the basketball team, and centre forward on the soccer team. Travelling to Manhattan on the subway from his home in Queens every day, he developed a rich kid's sophisticated irony, and a vicarious pleasure in low life. In a scene that could have come from *The Catcher in the Rye* he recalled how, on one occasion, "A man with a sign round his neck saying 'Deaf and Dumb' was shuffling past us on the train and someone called his bluff and goes: 'You're not deaf, you asshole' and just for a second I saw the guy react. That taught me a lot about New York City and what kind of phoniness there is around." He was also the kind of boy who used to amaze his parents' friends by multiplying and dividing incredibly large numbers in his head. For a while tennis was just something else he did well.

McEnroe's father began to develop an interest in

his son's game when they took lessons together at a club, when McEnroe was nine. His father used to joke that he "beat McEnroe two years running": when John was between the ages of nine and eleven. After that he watched, somehow always winning time off from the day job, rarely missing a match.

McEnroe's mother, Kay, was the driving force in the family. When her husband came in second in the state bar exam, she suggested that if he had worked a little harder he would have been first; when John got 95 percent in a test, she always enquired what had happened to the other 5 percent. Asked about her son's behaviour, she replied: "I suppose we always wanted a nice little Arthur Ashe, but we're very happy with what we've got. He's always had drive since he was a little fellow, always had to be first."

As the newspapers' fascination for psychobabble about McEnroe increased, reporters were dispatched to look for the secrets that had made him what he was. One zealous tennis correspondent believed he had found the answer to McEnroe's neurosis when he enquired of Kay if her son had ever been made to wash the dishes at home. "We have not been a chore-oriented house," she admitted solemnly, "which is my fault." McEnroe's mother entertained a hope that John might become a dentist (a therapist might have had something of a field day with that). When he adopted tennis as a career she rarely watched him play live, along with the rest of the world finding the experience almost too stressful.

His father, though, was a fixture at courtside, and was soon picked out by the cameras. From the beginning McEnroe occasionally found the paternal attention a little embarrassing, or at least unnerving: "Sometimes, I confess," he confessed, "I'd think 'Come on, take a break, take your wife out to lunch.' But [Dad] didn't seem to want to do anything else."

One of the effects of having to play out your whole life for the world in close proximity to your parents is that it becomes more difficult to be seen to grow up. The shock of McEnroe's anger was exaggerated for the viewer by the fact that the tantrums, as they came to be universally known, were performed in front of his father, the big-shot lawyer, who was forced to sit impotently and watch, usually in a comical white beanie hat that appeared not to belong to him. "I don't think I was spoiled," said McEnroe once, of his childhood, with a half-smile, "except that I always had what I wanted."

In his book *The Sibling Society*, Robert Bly, the American commentator, poet, and chest-thumping Iron John, described the modern process by which "adults regress towards adolescence and adolescents, seeing that, have no desire to become adults." This scenario, he suggested, resulted from the shift from a "paternal society" to one in which "impulse is given its way."

Bly detailed many factors contributing to this shift: permissiveness, and the advance of a style of parenthood that both encourages infantile choice-making and seeks personal affirmation from its children ("How could one be more clearly worthy of love than to agree with whatever your children want?"). Also cited were the feelings of inadequacy brought about by not having experienced war or national austerity (witness McEnroe's seismic clashes with the military heroes of the All England Club) and, added to that, the existence within society of a growing redundant ageing population, along with a widespread cynicism toward mentor figures of any kind.

The result was a generation of what Bly called "half-adults" intent on pursuing solipsistic fantasies, in love with the drama of their own emotions.

For perhaps many, or all, of these reasons, McEnroe, in common with much of the rest of young male Western society, always looked as if he were having a tough time working out how to grow up. In previous generations, tennis players, constricted by amateurism, had done other things—worked as PR executives for oil or tobacco companies, say—alongside playing tennis. Even the first Open generation of Ken Rosewall, Stan Smith, and Tony Roche looked like they had been playing just about forever. But, as money flooded the game, tennis players increasingly came to resemble the half-adults of Robert Bly's description. McEnroe, like all adolescents restless to be taken seriously, had looked forward to a coming of age, but having become world-famous for being a teen rebel at eighteen, the pressures on him, on and off court, to stay that way seemed to postpone the process. Certain tennis players, in particular his friend Vitas Gerulaitis, and Borg, had at least graduated from prodigies to "playboys." McEnroe seemed stuck at "Superbrat."

In some ways this limbo had been the story of his life. McEnroe started whacking around a plastic ball at eighteen months. In one of the family's earliest pieces of folklore, his father was throwing a ball to him as a toddler in Central Park when a lady approached and asked, "Is that a little boy or a midget?" At home McEnroe was called Junior. At school, because of his relatively diminutive size when he starred on the basketball team, he was Runt.

These taunts and the doubts they engendered seemed to plague him as he thought about turning pro. As late as 1977, when he was playing Ricardo Ycaza of Ecuador in the final of the WCT Junior tournament in Dallas, he caused a few headlines after breaking down and crying like a child on court when he lost. Later, in many of their matches, Connors would wind him up by calling him a baby at changeovers; sometimes, as he ate the Snickers bars and pulled at the fat Coke—the schoolboy's packed lunch he took on court in his bag— his lip appeared to be trembling. At Queens in 1979 he was fined a point before he had even started for not being ready when umpire Dick Lumb (a squadron leader, of course) called time; McEnroe was already arguing with the spectators. "I was wrong to say a few things to the crowd," he confessed afterwards. *"But they called me a baby,* and one lady said to me 'You're ugly.'"

Evidence that Britain's increasingly Bly-style society fetishised the young while apparently lacking patience or interest in the old or even the middle-aged was, by 1980, available everywhere. And one of the compelling attractions of McEnroe, again, was that he seemed effortlessly to dramatise that tension on court. "Old people shouldn't be umpires," he announced. "But who else wants to do it? It's a fact that old people don't see as well as young people."

He took a childish delight in showing up men who were his senior for their lack of sharpness. Fools were never suffered, and old fools were made to suffer. At the TransAmerica Open in San Francisco in 1981 McEnroe was playing against Bill Scanlon. He got up out of his seat at 6–6. He asked for a ball boy to throw him a tennis ball, then another, then another, and slowly he went round each of the half dozen ball boys on the court and asked them to surrender their balls to him. The umpire, fed up with this performance, called "Time" and warned

McEnroe that he was in danger of dropping a point. In response, one by one, McEnroe threw all the balls at the umpire: his way of reminding him that he had forgotten that new ones were overdue. "Time to change balls," he said, pointedly.

On court he thus demonstrated, along with Christopher Lasch's Psychological Man, the modern refusal to "subordinate the requirements of his feelings to others, or to some tradition outside the self." To the English, whose long-held traditions were threatened by the advancing me-culture, this was a crucial drama. The only other face that commanded so much of the media's attention in the summer of 1980 was that of Diana Spencer, who had been seen hiding behind a tree, Pan-like, in the company of Prince Charles, and revealed by the tabloids as a princess-in-waiting.

Diana was to become the high priestess of this child-within culture, but if she advanced herself as a role model for the sanctity of emotion over tradition, of a faith in "impulse" rather than "paternalism," then McEnroe was a more complicated icon. Always trusting his feelings, he was also frequently destructively overwhelmed by them.

I remember someone once comparing him at Wimbledon to one of those little boys in the stories of Maurice Sendak who sit down for their tea and then, because a single thing is out of place or a word has fallen wrong, find themselves adrift in a tempest of their own making, careering to the place Where the Wild Things Are. When I read those stories to my daughter now, it is impossible not to think of McEnroe, whose outbursts had just that quality of childlike intensity, not least because they seemed to appear out of nowhere. In arguing his case, too, he tended towards repetition ("Answer the question. I said *answer the question*"; "I want to see the referee. *Let* me see the referee"), the killer tactic of a child wearing down a desperate parent. In Sendak's fables, as in a toddler's screaming fit, when the Wild Things are tamed, tea can be resumed as if nothing had happened. McEnroe also seemed capable of this quality. Within seconds of his demons being leashed, he could be back at the service line, while everyone else on court, in particular his opponent, felt like they had been extras in the helicopter scene of *Apocalypse Now*.

McEnroe's hometown friend (and victorious mixed

doubles partner from the French Open of 1977) Mary Carillo once suggested of him that "so much of his graceless and disappointing behaviour comes from not looking beyond his own feelings." This inability to see the consequences of his emotions resulted in his recasting each tennis court he stepped on in his own image. "As the public world came to be seen as a mirror of the self," Lasch wrote, "people lost the capacity for detachment and hence for playful encounter, which presupposes a certain distance from the self."

McEnroe, for all his electric gifts, could not find that detachment. Throughout his autobiography, appropriately titled *You Cannot Be Serious* (or, in Britain, simply *Serious*), he says that the one thing he could never summon, and the thing that always most dismayed him, was that he could not express joy in what he did.

He knew, too, though, that while tennis allowed and increasingly required him to be a furious Peter Pan, there would have to come a time when he put aside childish things. "The magic of playing tennis for a living is that it lets you act like a kid for as long as you can keep going. But every kid has to grow up sometime," he said.

"Or wind up a case of arrested development." The ways in which McEnroe sought both to avoid and to address the implications of this fact in the two decades that followed his first Wimbledon final always seemed to me the most relevant—and compelling—sporting spectacle of our times.

# Number One

Lady Diana Spencer, who was to be married two weeks later, watched half the 1981 semifinal at Wimbledon from beneath her fringe. Just before McEnroe queried his eighth close line call, and suggested, in a scream, that either he or umpire George Grimes was "a disgrace to mankind," she had been whisked off for tea, her royal advisor perhaps fearing she might feel uncomfortable in the presence of charged emotion (little did he know). She missed, therefore, the last set of McEnroe's 7–6, 6–4, 7–5 victory over the unseeded Rod Frawley, his convincing mime of being garrotted, and his public warn-ing for unsportsmanlike behaviour.

From his opening match, when he had famously and repeatedly conjectured about the seriousness of the officialdom, and got into a long phenomenological de-bate about a handful of dust—"The ball was on the line! There was chalk!"—McEnroe had spent pretty much the whole fortnight arguing about arguing. ("I think I was wrong in what I said, but I felt justified in calling the linesman an incompetent fool.") Far from relishing the prospect of his rematch with Borg, the papers mostly wanted him deported. Several had taken to wheeling out media shrinks, for ongoing analysis of his state of mind. He was variously labelled an "hysterical extrovert" and a "petulant egomaniac." Even Mark Cox, the former British number one, now in the commentary box, of-fered his post-Jungian opinion on the nature of McEn-roe's particular condition, which required him, above all, he suggested, to "find a way of getting rid of *all that pent-up emotion.*"

In the press conference that followed the match, McEnroe was generously granted an opportunity to do just that. The first question, concerning his relationship with his girlfriend, Stacy Margolin, was perfectly designed to trigger the emotional release: "Have you and Stacy split up?"

The tactic worked admirably. McEnroe responded by saying, "You know, it's people like you who make me sick, all these papers here write such bullshit it's amazing. It's none of your business, first of all, and the answer is no. I mean I shouldn't even tell you no, because you are such trash anyway. . . . I want to say it, I'd like you to quote that you guys are shit. Can't you pick on somebody else, man? You got anyone else you can pick on? Talk about the match."

There was a short pause, in which that idea was considered, and then someone else, perhaps remembering the other person they had to pick on, said, "Can I ask one more question not about tennis?"

"No," said McEnroe.

"I'm here to cover Lady Diana," the reporter explained.

McEnroe looked more than usually pained. "Oh, I don't know. . . . She's a terrific person."

The members of the press giggled. McEnroe sat unblinking.

"But she's English," said the reporter, as if to help.

"That's just great," said McEnroe.

There was a longer pause. And then a dialogue developed, like a long baseline rally, onlookers' heads turning first to the player and then to the reporter.

Q: (SERVE) I believe during the match you made thirteen separate complaints. Would you say that each and every one of them was wholly and totally justified?

McEnroe: (FOREHAND) I don't even want to answer that question.

Q: (SLICED BACKHAND) Would you agree you made thirteen complaints?

McEnroe: (FOREHAND) I have no idea.

Q: (BACKHAND DOWN THE LINE) You have no idea, but do you feel they were all justified?

McEnroe: (BLOCKED FOREHAND) I have no idea.

Q: (CROSSCOURT BACKHAND) You have no idea whether they were justified?

**McEnroe:** (FOREHAND) I have no idea how many I made.

**Q:** (SCRAMBLED BACKHAND) Do you think that those you made were—

**McEnroe:** (FOREHAND APPROACH) What do you want me to say? That my underwear is purple? Give me a quote and I'll say it for you.

**Q:** (RUNNING BACKHAND) We think it is a tennis tournament—

**McEnroe:** (HALF-VOLLEY) I wish you'd write about it....

**Q:** (MISHIT BACKHAND) ...in which fairness—

**McEnroe:** (DROP SHOT) Why don't you be fair to me then?

**Q:** (RUNNING FOREHAND) ...should be looked after equally for both players—

**McEnroe:** (ANGLED VOLLEY) And it was unfair I questioned a call?

**Q:** (LOB) I think when it comes to thirteen complaints during the course of a match—

**McEnroe:** (STEPPING BACKWARDS) Only about nine were one hundred percent. (LAZY SMASH) Four were seventy-five percent.

This discussion went on for another ten or fifteen minutes. It was the closest they came to tennis, which was no longer really the story at all.

The following afternoon, John Barratt in the commentary box made a last-ditch attempt to summon up the Good Old Days. "There are signs that this could become quite a *noisy* match," he said, before fibbing a little. "And that's all to the good. One wants to see crowd involvement always," he went on. "The players like it. But we just hope there aren't some destructive people out there who might want to cheer mistakes and generally try to needle John McEnroe because," he said, "I think that might be unfortunate *for the whole game the world over.*"

We had been warned. Borg had almost clinched the first set while the commentary team was dwelling on how, this year, "there were to be no *banners* in the Centre Court, because a rivalry like that between McEnroe and Borg could *so easily* be inflamed unnecessarily." And then we were back with Mark Cox and his pent-up emotion.

The main reason for McEnroe's state of extreme, and infectious, nervous energy throughout that 1981

Wimbledon lay, he later claimed, in his growing belief that he had "got Borg's number," and his resultant fear that he would not make the advantage tell. After his Wimbledon defeat the previous year, McEnroe had beaten Borg in the 1980 US Open final, one of the very few times the Swede lost in five sets, and had repeated the feat earlier in 1981 in Milan. A win at Wimbledon would threaten Borg's number one status—which he had held for most of the past five years. In the winter McEnroe had turned down the opportunity to play a million-dollar one-off showdown against Borg in Sun City, South Africa, because "I thought I had better ways to make a million bucks." In March of that year they were photographed on the front of *World Tennis* magazine with duelling pistols and in frilly dress shirts, back to back.

Now that they were facing each other, McEnroe's advantage told in two tiebreaks, before he finally broke Borg in the fourth set, managing to hold his nerve and all that pent-up emotion, plus Self 1, in check. "A couple of times I said '*Come on!*' to myself and then said 'Don't even say that. Just use everything you have got for hitting the ball.'"

The story the next day was not about his victory,

though, or the end of Borg's reign, but the fact that he had missed the champions' dinner (or been disinvited, whichever tale you listened to). He had also been denied membership at the All England Club, the first champion in over a century to be refused that honour, due, said Sir Brian Burnett, "to Mr McEnroe's antics in the fortnight."

During the Wimbledon final Borg had used the tactic of coming into the net much more often than in the past, having allowed the doubt of the previous year to grow into a belief that he could not beat McEnroe with his usual game. Later that year he adopted the same ploy at the US Open, and when during the third set McEnroe passed him twice at the net and then hit two great looping lobs over his head, Borg seemed, for the first time in his career, to admit defeat. After the match he walked straight off court and into a car to the airport, missing the presentation ceremony. Three months after that he retired.

Several years later, when they were talking after an exhibition match, Borg said to McEnroe, in passing, "Number one is the only thing that matters. . . . You know it as well as I do. If you are number two, you might as well be number three or four. You're nobody."

There was always a certain closed society among the top ten players. Observing Boris Becker's arrival in that group, his coach explained that "when one of the top ten speaks, others keep quiet: that is the unwritten law. When Wilander talks about a tournament, no one else dares butt in. The top ten lead a secret life—and number one the most secret life of all. Number one goes into isolation, guarding and fostering the mystery around himself, trying to be an insoluble riddle. There is only one place number one has to lift the veil: on court."

For a long time Borg had maintained that mystery; he had beaten Connors ten times in a row. But McEnroe had seen through him, worked him out, and "got his number." Players dealt with that number one position in different ways. Borg had seemed born to it; Connors further bolstered his arrogance with it; Lendl used it as a consolation for choking in the biggest matches; Becker and Wilander, each having spent half a career getting there, couldn't summon the resolve to hold on to it. McEnroe, of course, needed it, and hated it. Isolation and mystery did not come easily to him, and mostly, in the three years he held on to the position, he said he had never felt so alone.

# Just Do It

#### seven

In 1977, a forty-year-old businessman sat in the crowd on Number One court at Wimbledon and watched the qualifier John McEnroe as he progressed in the main draw. The businessman was called Phil Knight and, as well as watching the tennis, he was looking for young players, especially young American players, who might wear his tennis shoes. Knight had been doing this kind of thing, on and off, for ten years or more, ever since, as a graduate of Stanford Business School (and as a reasonably good track athlete), he had decided that there must be a way of making running shoes that did not hurt your feet. He had founded a company called Blue Ribbon, imported $500 worth of prototype trainers from Japan, and started attending athletics meetings, selling the trainers from the back of his car. By 1977, at the suggestion of one of his employees, Knight had changed the name, slightly against his better judgement, to Nike (he had wanted to call it Dimension 6). Nike had needed a logo, and he paid a designer friend $25 to come up with one: a chubby sort of tick he called a swoosh.

Knight had an idea that he might invest his little swoosh with an attitude. That afternoon on Court One he thought he might have found just the attitude he had been looking for. After the match, Knight contacted the eighteen-year-old McEnroe and offered him a contract to wear Nike tennis shoes. Three years later, Nike was the biggest sportswear brand in the world. A decade after that, the billionaire Phil Knight could sit in his office, called the Wimbledon Room, on the top floor of the John McEnroe Building at his headquarters in Portland, Oregon, and claim with some justification to have the world at his feet.

In talking of what he had seen in McEnroe, Knight

said he could identify a spirit that matched something he wanted both in his company and in its products. "Mac" was "a fearless athlete," he explained, who "set new standards of intensity and desire to win." As Donald Katz points out in his biography of Nike, Knight was looking not just for winners, but for winners who lived by their own rules: "The kind of athletes that embarrass grown-ups were entirely acceptable Nike guys." Knight saw players like McEnroe as "modern saints" who embodied our new faith in self-expression and self-creation. If you bought a Nike shoe you were also, the theory went, buying into something of that antiestablishment spirit. "Remember, tennis is the sport with a scoring system that was specifically designed to keep the commoners from understanding what was going on—'deuce,' 'love' and all that; it was an elitist code," argued Nike's "Tennis Maven," and former pro, Ian Hamilton. "Mac broke that code everywhere he could."

Sometimes the power of that code-breaking appeal could be measured directly in dollars. At Wimbledon in 1985, for example, after stepping on a ball and twisting his ankle, McEnroe experimented by playing on Centre

Court wearing a racquetball shoe, which had a high ankle support. A modest ten thousand of these shoes had been bought in the previous year. By the end of 1985 that figure was more than a million. Most often, though, the benefits of "the *idea* of McEnroe" to the brand were intangible, and not confined to the sale of tennis attire.

Knight believed that the desire that sportsmen like McEnroe (and later Michael Jordan and Tiger Woods) displayed in their game reflected a new attitude in society. The attitude became enshrined in a series of Nike slogans, the most effective and memorable of which was "Just Do It." On one level the phrase served to dramatise the actions of the player on court. McEnroe may have been trapped in his eternal internal dialogue, but his game offered him a way out. He could cut through all the angst, stop being Psychological Man, and just play. (It was a happy coincidence, too, that those very qualities Knight could project in McEnroe were also the qualities of an ideal consumer: perpetually dissatisfied, restless, and constantly seeking personal gratification. That consumer, faced with the question of whether to spend

$150 on another pair of shoes to enhance his image of himself as an antiestablishment man of action, was given a built-in answer to his own anxiety: "Just Do It.")

Nike became a model for the 1980s and 1990s economy because it did not make products; it sold emotions. The emotion was borrowed from the icons around whom the company spirit was built, and the original icon was John McEnroe. The brand, like the player, polarised people. What Knight wanted was an image that people felt strongly about, whether they loved it or hated it. The success of the business, he said, lay in "all the emotion we generate and the tremendous well of emotion we live off of."

Just as people's clothing once identified them as belonging to a particular class, so, in the 1980s, and particularly in America, did branded sports shirts and sneakers cement their allegiances to a particular corporate culture. Nike shoes may have been sold to the accompaniment of words by William S. Burroughs and music by Gil Scott-Heron ("The revolution will not be televised"), but the message, when allied to sporting success, was a new kind of winning. For the entrepreneurs and their employees in the emergent New Economy, based on America's West Coast, rebellion was the new corporate style. As early as 1975, in his study of American business practices, *Routes to the Executive Suite,* the business writer Emerson Jennings had observed how "The new upwardly mobile corporate executive does not view himself as an organisation man." His "anti-organisational posture" in fact "has emerged as his chief characteristic. He advances through the corporate ranks not by serving the organisation but by convincing his associates that he possesses the attributes of a winner."

Nike was intent on suggesting to each individual in its global public that he or she could play, in this way, at work and in society, like McEnroe: by no rules but his or her own. The brand, then, defined not so much a company as a way of life, a "cult" even, and on its "World Campus" it practised what it preached. All new employees were "oriented" with a video of sporting epiphanies—McEnroe's 1981 Wimbledon was one—which came with a motivational sound track about the unflinching competitive soul of the athlete. They were provided, too, with a new language. Managers on the Nike Campus were "coaches," designers who achieved promotion were "player coaches," meetings were "huddles," and employees' careers were measured from "sprinter" to "long-distance runner."

Loyalty to the brand was stressed above all else. During team-building sessions, Knight would arrange for McEnroe to come to the campus and play a little tennis against him. (The two men wore microphones and talked to the coaches about the glories of Nike's global mission as they hit the ball around.) Tennis lessons, and other sporting contests, were scheduled into the working day. "People take it very much in earnest," one employee noted in 1987; "I was on [a company] Ultimate Frisbee team—I thought just for fun—and there was this one woman from the marketing department who used to push and shove and just bite my head off when I didn't take it super-seriously."

Witnessing Nike's success, and as the New Economy boomed, other corporations started to adopt these kinds of practices. But just as work was becoming more like sport, so too was sport becoming more like work. "Nike always felt sports shouldn't have boundaries," Knight suggested, alive to the commercial possibilities of that position. And so, while businessmen played out fantasies of being tennis players or basketball stars, tennis players began to see themselves as businessmen.

This seemed to me—keen, I suppose, to keep faith in the idea of the game—to have a dramatic effect on the way it was played, even by McEnroe. From very early in his career he was fond of saying: "Tennis is big business, and there is nothing very gentlemanly about that." He shared the philosophy of the new breed of commodities brokers and bond dealers in that: "I don't want to hang on in the game like Arthur Ashe, I want to make my money and get out." As in corporate life, it became hard, when earning several million dollars a year, not to believe that in some way you deserved to be earning several million dollars a year. To support this sense of self-worth, McEnroe, like all players, became a little industry in himself, surrounded by a travelling team of PR men and agents who decided where their product should best be placed. "As Connors's career wound down," McEnroe observed later, "he would say in interviews 'I'm a businessman.' And I'd be thinking: 'What business is he in?' He's in the business of endorsing products! I'd think *'Hey, I'm a businessman, too!'* "

In his classic study of the history of play, *Homo Ludens*, the cultural historian Johann Huizinga argued that, in our times, "A far-reaching contamination of play and serious activity has taken place. The two spheres are getting mixed. In activities of an outwardly serious nature hides an element of play. Recognised play, on the other hand, is no longer able to maintain its true play character as a result of being taken too seriously and being technically over-organised. The indispensable qualities of detachment, artlessness, and gladness are thus lost."

This kind of shift was very much apparent, by the late 1970s, in the dressing rooms of Wimbledon. Gordon Forbes, who at the peak of his career once beat the great Lew Hoad at a tournament in the United States and won a casserole dish, recalled walking through the players' lounge at Wimbledon in 1978 and hearing words that once would never have been mentioned before a match. Whereas in his time the talk had been primarily about who was playing well, and who was worth watching in the ladies' draw, now all the conversation was of "things like 'contracts,' 'franchises,' 'legal representatives,' and 'twelve point five million by May.' . . . Oh, there are new kinds of people in tennis these days," he suggested, "especially in the States. Social sort of people who have heard that it is fashionable to 'have trouble with your forehand.' They quickly get equipped with Fila gear and several rackets, teaching pros and phrases like 'topspin lob' and 'punch volley' and 'hitting through the netman.' And if, after lessons, they can't play well with the Wilson steel, they can try the Kawasaki graphite, or the Head aluminium, or Boron XT or Durafiber or Glaflex. And if they still have problems actually playing, it isn't important, because they have the tennis talk and the trappings, and afterwards they can put on 'après tennis' gear, and do fun."

Doing fun, the product of the oxymoronic leisure industry, was fast becoming the biggest business of all. Nike, said Phil Knight, was "about much more than business—[it was] a company with a soul." You might say that a good part of that soul had been transplanted wholesale from the sports it colonised. One of the triumphs of the sports marketing conglomerates was to ally the progress of the game with new technologies. Once equipment started to define attitude and proficiency on court then it followed that there would always be the latest technical advancement—the latest racket, the latest shoes—to buy, to give the winner an edge.

McEnroe's 1981 victory over Borg was the last Wimbledon won with a wooden racket. After the arrival of the large-head rackets in the early 1980s tennis equipment was sold, like pretty much everything else, as if it was a branch of space-age technology. The most convincing way of measuring this advance was in the pace and power of service, the extra miles per hour that graphite added to your game. As a result tennis became yet another of our dreams of velocity.

The oddest thing now—I almost said *saddest*—when watching the finals of 1980 and 1981 is the way in which Borg and McEnroe had, comparatively, for all their effortless speed around court, so much time to construct their rallies. Their rackets look insubstantial, almost, not the vicious bats of today. In many respects these finals marked the watershed years of tennis and Wimbledon—the last time when genuine subtlety and guile, the attributes that McEnroe preserved, could honestly compete with the obdurate power hitting that, ironically, Borg promoted and which quickly became the game's trademark.

It is an age-old tennis fantasy to have players of different eras line up against each other: how would Fred Perry have fared against Rod Laver? How would Bill Tilden have coped with Connors? And so on. In a way, the racket technology which contributed to making absolute dedication and seriousness a prerequisite of anyone in the top one hundred made this kind of speculation redundant. All of those players would beat Roy Emerson or Lew Hoad or Pancho Gonzales. The game they were playing was different not just in spirit but in kind.

With the arrival of corporate millions most other sports had flirted with these kinds of advances. In soccer there were for a while artificial pitches. Dennis Lillee, the volatile Australian cricketer, abandoned the traditional willow bat and came out a few times with an aluminum one. But only tennis, it seemed to me, had allowed the changes to affect the game materially (the ability of golfers, able to hit the ball farther with "metal woods," was countered by longer courses). In 1985 Bjorn Borg made a brief and unsuccessful comeback from retirement with his wooden Donnay racket and found himself competing against a different sport entirely, one that owed far more to power and spin than to touch or quickness of instinct. Faced with this new game, McEnroe, you might say, had, indirectly, begun to argue himself out of a career. (Not surprisingly, in a recent list of the things he would change if he were in charge of tennis, paramount was "a return to wooden rackets. . . . Wood to me has glamour. You need strategy and technique. Tennis these days is sadly lacking in those things. It's all, as David Bowie said, 'Wham, bam, thank you ma'am.' ")

In place of glamour, tennis suddenly had technology, and in place of sportsmen, it had personalities. Martin Amis once suggested that "personalities" in tennis, as in "whatever happened to the personalities?," were generally synonymous with "a seven-letter duosyllable starting with an 'a' and ending with an 'e' (and also featuring, in order of appearance, an 'ss', an 'h', an 'o', and an 'l')." He saw the direct lineage of "personalities" running through Nastase and Connors to McEnroe and Agassi.

In the early years of McEnroe's career it always looked to me that the "antics" of Nastase (who routinely called Arthur Ashe "negroni" and once "nigger") and Connors (simulating masturbation with his racket handle) were different from McEnroe's outbursts, far more calculated, less real. McEnroe had, I thought, what he modestly called in his autobiography "anger, presence, integrity" because he always appeared subject to forces that he could barely contain and was unable quite to understand.

As his career developed, however, he seemed in danger of becoming more the thing that the tabloids and the corporations wanted him to be. In 1980 he was arguing, "I have never been fined for saying anything obscene. It's always something like 'you are the pits.' Is that the most unbelievable thing that has ever been?" But by 1991 the stakes of rebellion had been raised. At Wimbledon in 1991 he was heard to tell a linesman, "Good fucking call, you son of a fucking bitch. You fucking report me after the match and I'll fucking . . ."

This attitude had, for more than a decade, been endorsed and branded. During the 1980s, in pressing to find the limits of what he and his "personality" could get away with, McEnroe had suggested that on occasion he "wanted" to be defaulted from a tournament, just to show himself where the boundaries were. The great irony was that—because the marketing of tennis for television was based increasingly on his "personality"—

if he was sent home, the money went home, too: "The tournament directors knew it, the umpires (who got paid by the tournament) knew it, the linesmen knew it," he said. "And I knew it." This knowledge fed the megalomania that he sought to tame. "The more that professional tennis's money depended on me, the more things seemed to be under my control when I got out on court."

Ironically in these circumstances the instinctive imperative, Just Do It, began, on occasion, to look more and more like a kind of posturing, the actions that a man might play. Nike graced Sunset Boulevard with a vast James Dean–like mural of McEnroe on a city street, the collar of his leather jacket turned up. It looked like a lot to live up to. Whereas his rage had once possessed him, now he seemed apt to try to summon it, locked, you might say, into the personality Nike had given him. There was not just his volatile self to think of, there was the integrity of the brand, too. And there was plenty riding on that integrity. Knight was said by those close to him to be "far more despondent over John McEnroe's loss at Wimbledon in 1982 than were McEnroe's father or even McEnroe." And not without good reason: in some ways he had more to lose, not least a $300 million a year tennis shoe business.

The worst thing about the amount of money that now attended "personality" was that other "personalities" also began to emerge. These wannabe McEnroes included some very good players, notably Pat Cash, Wimbledon winner in 1987, who was anxious to play up the similarities between himself and his friend, arguing that "we were two of the sport's most notorious outlaws. . . . Of Irish descent and both men of passion." One of the things to like about John McEnroe, however, was that he was not Pat Cash: "Growing up I'd always seen myself as just a normal Aussie kid who liked rock and roll music, football and girls, but I suppose I was just a little bit left of centre." Cash established his personality by climbing up the courtside to his friends and family after his Wimbledon victory. "I don't know if anyone tried to stop me," he said. "If they did, too bad." When he reached the box, setting a trend for future tournaments, he embraced his mentor, Ian Barclay: "We fucking did it, Barkers, we fucking did it!"

Other players simply substituted personality for talent. Chief among these was Jeff Tarango, a middle-ranking player. In a typical scene the volatile Californian was playing Alexander Mronz at Wimbledon in 1995 and was aggrieved when a serve he thought was an ace was called out. When the crowd whistled he told them to shut up, and the umpire issued a code violation. Tarango flew into an uncontrollable rage and then stormed off court, defaulting the match, after suggesting: "You are the most corrupt official. I'm not playing anymore." As the umpire made his way back to the changing room, he encountered Bénédicte Carrière, Tarango's wife, who slapped him across the face. Later she defended her action by suggesting: "If Jeff had done it, he would have been put out of tennis."

For a long while Andre Agassi laboured, too, with this kind of image. As McEnroe's game was waning at the end of the 1980s, Nike swung the full force of their branding operation behind Agassi (who had starred on their Nike Junior Team as a twelve-year-old alongside Jim Courier). He turned professional in a blaze of hype at sixteen, but by the age of twenty-one he seemed already strung out, eating badly, losing games for fun, his ever-changing appearance apparently reflecting his fragile self-esteem: first he shaved his head, then grew a tall

Mohawk, then bleached it, before finally settling on a shaggy shoulder-length highlighted perm.

At one tournament in Florida, when in his teens, he turned up on court wearing cutoff jeans, lipstick, and eyeliner. Looking back on that time, he reflected that "maybe I was rewarded too quickly. I came at a time when tennis needed somebody—when tennis was looking for another American. I had so much notoriety before I had really accomplished great things. For me to be doing Nike commercials and never winning a Grand Slam—that left me with a bad rap—all image and no substance." ("At least," remarked Connors, "in our day we used to win.")

As anticorporate activist Naomi Klein argued in her book *No Logo*, more than any other company Nike sought "to erase all boundaries between the sponsor and the sponsored." In some cases they were almost entirely successful. "I'm Nike's guy," Andre Agassi said bluntly in 1992. "I grew up with this chemistry they can create. We grew up into a personality we made together. We have a history." It was, he might have added, a history that guaranteed him $100 million, over a decade, simply for wearing a shirt.

During the course of McEnroe's career the money that was available in the game suddenly began to reflect the money that was now available in upper reaches of the New Economy. For his 1980 Wimbledon final against Bjorn Borg, McEnroe collected $14,000 as runner-up. A teacher in Britain at that time was earning about that as an annual salary, a junior doctor nearly twice that. By 1984, though, McEnroe could shout at a crowd, "I'm worth forty thousand of you," and—still expert at doing those big multiples in his head—mean it. By the time of his last competitive match at the Grand Slam Cup in Munich, each player received $120,000 just to turn up, and the winner took home a cheque for $2.3 million, an amount, said McEnroe, "so sickening it made me want to vomit."

The money did not come without a price. The Grand Slam was the end-of-season inducement to players to compete in as many tournaments across the world as possible during the year to accumulate points. "Initially," McEnroe says, he resisted it for this reason. "I stayed away, as did Andre, Boris, and Mats [Wilander]. But what have we had in return? Nothing. They just want us to play more and more events. So I'd rather go there, take the money, and give it to people who really need it."

The expansion of the tour in the early 1980s, and the mandatory requirement of the players to follow much of it, meant an endless season. No other sport required its stars to travel halfway across the globe on a weekly basis to fulfil sponsors' contracts. The sports companies and their TV advertisers liked to have their players competing in emerging markets (Phil Knight always loved the fact that in a poll of rural Chinese regarding men who had shaped the century, Michael Jordan came third behind Chairman Mao and Zhou Enlai). One of the effects of this itinerary was a dilution of the magic of the great events. The top players met each other so often that a Wimbledon or a US Open was just one more final among many. Another was that conditioning, and a kind of robotic mental strength, pioneered by Ivan Lendl, became the dominant spirit, the only way to survive.

"They are trying to turn us into money whores. It's obscene," McEnroe was suggesting in 1990, somewhat after the event. Boris Becker, who at the age of twenty was worth maybe $30 million, and had turned down perhaps the same again in endorsements, explained how: "They say 'a million.' And then you say 'No.' And then they offer—because they think everyone has his price—three million. And then you say 'No' again. At least it feels good to know I don't come cheap."

Even this, though, was small change to the likes of Phil Knight. From his original $500 investment in track shoes, Knight was, by the time McEnroe retired, included in the growing "over $1,000,000,000 category" on *Forbes* magazine's annual rich list. He was asked in 1992, by one journalist at the Barcelona Olympics, whether he thought "Nike creates images for athletes that exceed their capacity to perform as athletes—or as real people." He thought for a moment. "My short answer is yes," he said. "But it's not just us. It's TV that really defines these athletes. We just expand on the image. But perhaps our efforts do combine with the power of television to come together and create something that nobody can live up to."

# "There Goes 1987"

## eight

"I would like to reach my potential just one time in my life," John McEnroe said at the beginning of 1984. By which time, it seemed to me, he had already begun ticking off a fair few of Cyril Connolly's Enemies of Promise: those impediments to sustained great work that afflict both writers and, I'd have argued, tennis players alike.

McEnroe had succumbed, for example, to the clamour of early success (which, Connolly suggested, "raises his standard of living, lowers his standard of criticism and encourages the germ of its opposite, failure"), reaching the Wimbledon semifinals just before he was due to take up his scholarship at Stanford University, earning a quarter of a million dollars in his first three months on the tour, and winning the US Open by the time he was twenty. (In novelist's terms, this was his *Catch-22*.) He had been caught, too, in the snares of journalism, though in his case more as a victim of its "loose intimacies" than their author (his *Bonfire of the Vanities*). And although he mostly avoided drink (Connolly's "substitute for art"), he had dabbled ("fatal self-forgetfulness") in drugs: as early as 1979 he was appearing in Andy Warhol's diaries as Vitas Gerulaitis's sidekick at the cocaine-fuelled New York clubs Studio 54 and Xenon, by which time, Warhol notes, Gerulaitis had taken to "wearing his gold coke-cutter razor blade around his neck during matches" (his *Bright Lights, Big City*).

The remaining two seductions from immortality (sex, "crippling demands on his time and money," and domesticity, "the pram in the hallway") were still accidents waiting to happen. In the meantime, for a brief spell, McEnroe set about securing his legend. If he had been a novelist, 1984 would have been, well, his *1984* year. His 6–1, 6–1, 6–2 destruction of Jimmy Connors in the Wimbledon final was perhaps the most imperious performance in tennis history. McEnroe put 78 percent of his first serves in, more than half of which Connors, then the most effective returner of serve in the game, failed even to get a proper racket on. And he backed up that service with near faultless volleys and ground-strokes, making only three unforced errors in the match. There was no doublespeak, nothing much to curse. And though he didn't quite manage happy, in the papers he was suddenly Saint John.

He went on to avenge his Paris defeat by Lendl (and the crackling headphones) at the US Open, and by the end of the year he had played seventy-eight singles matches and lost only two. Still, though, he had a sense of profound dissatisfaction. Having drifted through the previous two years "in an odd state of mourning for Borg," his old nemesis came back to haunt him in December: the ghost of Christmas past with a two-fisted backhand. In a semifinal in Stockholm against the dogged Swede Anders Jarryd, McEnroe was fined for calling the umpire a jerk and for hitting a soda can so it sprayed over the King of Sweden, who was sitting at courtside (all the while, he remembered thinking: "Where is Borg?"

and "Who is Jarryd?"). Waiting to get on a flight to L.A. as the Open champion and the world number one—a position he had now held, with little pleasure, for three years—he asked himself, with characteristic modesty: "I'm the greatest player who ever lived. Why do I feel so empty inside?"

By the beginning of 1985, McEnroe was increasingly looking beyond the game to find the answer to this question. At a party in the Hollywood Hills, thrown by Alana Stewart (Rod's ex, whom McEnroe had reportedly been dating), he thought he had located the solution across a crowded room in the eyes of Tatum O'Neal.

I once asked Andre Agassi what had attracted him to the child star Brooke Shields (they sent each other faxes for nearly a year before they really met each other and eventually got married) and he suggested that she'd had an even weirder childhood than he had. As a result, he said, she was, like him, both grown up and not grown up. McEnroe found something of the same thing in O'Neal.

"She was successful even younger than me," he explained, "and I felt she could help me to navigate what it would be like to be in the public eye, which I was having some troubles with. She was only twenty-two years old when she had the first of our three kids, so looking back it seems strange that we did not feel at the time that we were in way over our heads. But when you are young you feel you can do it all. Or at least we did."

O'Neal, of course, had won her Oscar for *Paper Moon* at the age of ten. Five years later, she had been left to her own devices in Hollywood, looking after her younger brother in the absence of her drug-dependent mother and womanising father. When Kenneth Tynan met her around this time, she was, he suggested, "going on 38." He later related the conversation they'd had to Laurence Olivier:

KT: (BREAKING THE ICE)  Good evening, Tatum.

**Tatum:** Mnnh.

KT: I suppose you know everyone in this room, don't you?

**Tatum:** Ymnh.

KT: Is there anyone in the world that you don't know that you would like to meet?

**Tatum:** (PAUSE)  Nah.

KT: Maybe Laurence Olivier?

**Tatum:** (PONDERS DEEPLY A MOMENT. LONG PAUSE. THEN SHAKES HER HEAD) Nah.

Five years after that, five more years of partying and drug-taking, it is hard to imagine that Tatum O'Neal could be surprised by anyone, but McEnroe looked, she said, like someone she had never seen before. She responded, as tennis fans responded, as Nike consumers responded, to his "realness." And he, in turn, saw in her something he lacked. Looking back, he suggested it was not so much Tatum that attracted him, but "Tatum in her element," and her element was a star-studded, druggy milieu.

That world—if not the drugs—was addictive. "I'd like to challenge anyone that would not be kind of intoxicated by all of that," he said when I interviewed him, bright eyed, of his subsequent A-list life. "And Tatum was very comfortable with that place. She'd come through a lot already and was looking to become independent from her family, and I thought I could help her with that. That was the idea at the time. And at the time it was impossible not to feel, like, *wow*, this is all incredible."

With Tatum on his arm, McEnroe got to hang out

with even more of his heroes: Jack Nicholson and Mick Jagger, both of whom offered him similar advice after he'd been banned from the Davis Cup for his behaviour in 1985: don't ever change. ("When you're twenty-six, who are you gonna listen to," he wondered, "Jagger and Nicholson or some old farts in the United States Tennis Association?")

Some of the partying produced in him "guilt and exhilaration all mixed up. You could be out with these guys, and you'd be having a wonderful time and you'd constantly be thinking you had to get your head back to the tennis. . . . I'd like to think I'm an athlete at heart, and I knew you can't burn both ends of the candle. Maybe it's being brought up a Catholic, but you realise pretty quickly that it is going to interfere with things."

(While McEnroe is coy about his own drug-taking, part of him is anxious about whether it affected his game. "It didn't help," he says. "If you go out and have marijuana or whatever, I suppose that's not going to help you maintain the right energy level in the fifth set. Of course not.")

He had felt uncomfortable with his celebrity from the moment in 1977 that he reached the semifinals at

Wimbledon; he returned home, to find himself, as he recalls, a "somebody" and his friends still "nobodies." He once suggested that if any player could buy his privacy then he would do so, not realising, or not wanting to realise, that exposure was the quid pro quo of the television-sponsored millions: that was the deal. "How much money do [the media] want to leave us alone?" he asked. "We'd all pay up to be left alone, but I don't see any of you giving us our privacy. The type of people who do that for a living will end up in a miserable place," he said, hopefully. "Their karma will get them eventually."

McEnroe had tried arguing with the press, attacking it, and inviting it into his home. Tatum, who had grown up with all this, looked like she might provide a new way to protect him from it all: they could be in it together, for the long haul, like Madonna and Sean or Tom and Nicole. At the very least, she would never "act like a fan."

One of the attractions for McEnroe, and the ultimate aphrodisiac, you might imagine, in the "culture of Narcissism," was that seeing Tatum was like looking in the mirror. "She reminded me of a female version of myself. The best parts," he said. And: "I thought Tatum was a diamond in the rough, that I was going to be the guy to polish her up and help her shine."

His first serious girlfriend, Stacy Margolin, had been a Californian tennis player with a degree in psychology, which, on occasion, probably helped. They bonded, she said, in part because they liked the same food: "Chinese, Italian, popcorn, and home-blended fruit drinks." Stacy Margolin, though, was not a young woman who would, say, have invited Michael Jackson back to her room (as, by Jacko's account, Tatum did) in an attempt to relieve him of his virginity.

Neither, perhaps, would she have suggested that she and McEnroe consummate their celebrity fairy tale at the house of her "wicked stepmother," Farrah Fawcett. The night in question was freezing cold, McEnroe remembered, and they were in the neighbourhood, and Farrah and Ryan were away. . . . The "Why nots?" might presumably have included the fact that Farrah was his adolescent pinup, and it was Tatum's extreme relationship with her father that was behind many of her frailties. In any case, McEnroe, who had faced down the psychological challenge of Borg and Lendl and Becker, discovered that he did not have the mental toughness for this particular occasion. "[It was] the combination of the cold and the weird buzz . . . ," he claimed, limply.

Despite this, a year later McEnroe and O'Neal ("Brat and Brat" for the *National Enquirer*) were married and had had their first child. And, to quote Jack Nicholson in *As Good As It Gets*, for a while it seemed Tatum made McEnroe "want to be a better man."

In 1980 someone asked Vitas Gerulaitis if he thought getting married would make any difference to Borg's play. "I hope so," he replied.

The example of Borg and Mariana had worried McEnroe. When Connors married former Playboy Play-mate of the Month Patti McGuire, McEnroe used to sug-gest to friends that Jimbo had lost his sense of fun, and that he spent too much time with his wife. "Which is," he said to Borg, just before their 1980 Wimbledon, "also going to happen to you, my dear."

Now a part of him feared it was about to happen to him, too. It had started at Wimbledon in 1985, when he had pulled out of his usual warm-up tournament, Queens, because he could not face the press hound-ing him about Tatum. Then, less prepared than usual, he lost to the South African Kevin Curren in straight sets.

Having felt for so long a boy, now, he said, blown off court by Curren, he suddenly "felt very old out there."

This sense of diminishing opportunity only served to exaggerate his behaviour on court, and began to express itself, for some people, in the way that McEnroe actually played the game. Günther Bosch, Boris Becker's coach, in his book about the mental side of tennis, suggested that "when you lose your cool, you can't think. When it happens to McEnroe these days, he suddenly starts playing from the baseline, stops going up to the net. Psychologists would be interested to note that players do the opposite of where their strength lies. They start playing against themselves."

And McEnroe now had several more selves to play against. There was the self who still dreamed of fulfilling his potential, just once; there was the self who felt he ought to be at home with Tatum and the family, the evangelical new man; and there were the several old selves who told him, by turns, that he was throwing away his genius, or that maybe he had done enough and was through with the game.

In this frame of mind he came to face Brad Gilbert at the Masters. Gilbert was a trier, which always annoyed

McEnroe because, as he noted without irony, "he was so down on everything, and he'd bring you down, too." When he started to lose, McEnroe informed his opponent at changeover: "Gilbert, you don't deserve to be on the same court with me!" And then, when he was facing defeat: *"You are the worst! The fucking worst!"* After the loss McEnroe announced that he was going on what turned out to be a seven-month sabbatical, to be with his family, because "when I start losing to players like him, I've got to start reconsidering what I'm doing even playing this game."

He believed, meanwhile, that his parents did not approve of Tatum, because they felt he was destroying his career over her. His sensitivity to this was perhaps heightened because it reflected his own fears. In any case, he recalled, it caused him to clash with the mother who always wondered where the missing 5 percent was in his school exams. When he explained to her he was considering returning to tennis after his layoff she said: "Now you can buy some diapers for Kevin."

He replied: "Mom, how much is enough? Tell me. How much money do I have to make before you don't have to say things like that? Give me a specific number.

Is it five million? Ten? Fifteen? Twenty? Tell me a number, so when I make it I won't have to hear about this anymore!"

When his and Tatum's marriage began to go wrong, some of it had to do with her self-destructive impulses. But, as McEnroe said, "You know she had three kids in five years, and this is where it got really difficult for us." From O'Neal's point of view, though, it was a result of McEnroe's difficulties in combining fatherhood with his waning dreams of greatness on court, his stubborn and multiplying enemies of promise. When she announced she was pregnant with their second son, his first response was to say, simply, "There goes 1987" and, though he later regretted it, to wonder if she might get an abortion.

When, subsequently, McEnroe got knocked out in the first round of the US Open in 1986 by Paul Annacone, the kind of player he used to slice and dice for fun, he wondered if anything was worth it. "It's dark inside my head. Unfortunately there's no light switch I can use. For eight or nine years the light was bright for me, then it flickered a bit; maybe I'm at the point where Bjorn Borg finished with tennis."

In fact, McEnroe continued, on and off, for several more years, lured by the rewards as much as anything, but he never reached another Grand Slam singles final, and remained adamant that his wife should be at home with their three kids while he toured. "The one thing that stayed the same for me, for a long time, was the money," he said. "The money made things very complicated. . . . I chose world-class mediocrity for the last five or six years of my career. I couldn't just walk away from that kind of money."

At the age of twenty-seven it looked to me like he'd probably added a new item to Cyril Connolly's list of demons: the premature end of dreams of omnipotence. "When you are young you feel invulnerable," he said. "I don't feel invulnerable anymore."

# The Lines

#### nine

In the spring of 2001 I was sitting opposite the then reigning US Open champion, the giant Russian Marat Safin, in the players' lounge at the annual Masters tennis tournament in the high desert air of Palm Springs, and wondering what to say. I had flown here to interview Safin for a magazine article and, after being variously informed over the course of several days by his sponsors and agents and managers and promoters that arrangements had changed, and were still changing, and that

Marat "needed his focus," I finally had been granted a precious half hour with him.

There are certain subjects that professional tennis players, these days, will not really talk about in interviews. These subjects include any aspect of their interior life, their relationships with other players, romance, money, emotions, politics, and ideas. The things they will talk about, in their place, generally involve the current trajectory of their ball toss, and the particular degree of their intensity for the coming match. They can do this at some length.

Among the press corps who sit in the mandatory postmatch interviews, Safin was considered something of an exception to this rule. Numbed veterans of a thousand quote-free Q & As with Greg Rusedski ("he raised his level at a crucial time") or Lindsay Davenport ("I raised my level at a crucial time") had informed me that the Russian—who had doled out irony and vodka to the hacks after his victory in Flushing Meadows—was something of a raconteur.

The distinction, I was finding, however, was a fine one. Having watched Safin practise for a couple of days, I had been struck by the way in which, for all his power and skill, he seemed somehow absent from the process of hitting the ball. He carried that same sense in person, too, apparently barely able to bring himself to think about tennis, let alone talk about it.

Safin's story was typical of the new breed of players. He is the son of parents who ran what was once Moscow's only tennis club. He began playing when he could walk and moved, alone, to Spain to play tennis pretty much full-time when he was twelve. At the age of twenty-one, he lived as a tax exile in Monte Carlo, along with half the other top-ranked players. A couple of years earlier, after a run of poor results, he had thought about giving up tennis, because he couldn't find any motivation or satisfaction in it. Now, though, he had established himself in the top ten for two years running and conservative estimates put his consequent wealth at nearly $20 million. This was, perhaps, motivation and satisfaction enough.

As we talked, some of the reasons for Safin's apparent indolence in Palm Springs became clear. He was at this tournament, one of eight mandatory Masters Series events, with a severe back injury that required him to wear a medieval-looking brace around his chest. The rules were such, however, that if he did not play the tournament, even if injured, he would probably not qualify for the end-of-season cash handout in the Masters final.

Though he was too smart to say as much, he was here, therefore, simply in order to guarantee his share of the pot. And although the tennis authorities would not say so, either, they were happy to preside over a situation that effectively blackmailed the world's second-best player to risk his season, and conceivably his career, to allow them to have his name on the Palm Springs posters and keep their sponsors happy.

The following day, in front of an entirely uninterested crowd, I watched Safin pat-ball serves at 70 mph and barely move from the spot in losing easily to a player ranked a hundred places below him. I wondered what McEnroe would have made of it. *Glamour* and *intensity*, or even *sport* and *competition*, were not words that sprang to mind.

Later I asked Safin if he managed to find enough distractions in Monte Carlo.

He laughed a little: "I try to do my best to have fun off the court," he said. "You are only twenty-one once. You cannot make big parties, you cannot take cocaine or whatever, obviously, but there are plenty of other ways of having fun."

Such as?

"Oh, I buy cars," he said. "Cars, cars, cars, so many cars."

Did he ever find it hard to find the enthusiasm to play?

He looked around the room, smiled at his compatriot Yevgeny Kafelnikov, who was playing pool. (Kafelnikov, though worth $35 million, had recently been complaining that tennis players were not properly rewarded for their efforts.) "No," said Safin finally, "it's not hard to concentrate. It's all business to me and this tennis business is a business I like very much."

Oddly, the impression that I came away with from meeting Safin was that he was trapped in a world that seemed vaguely absurd to him. (Some of this frustration seemed to come out in his game. At the end of his first year on the tour Safin admitted to having broken forty-eight rackets in anger, more than one per tournament. So anxious were the tennis authorities to encourage this kind of "personality" in the game, these days, however, that they duly relaxed the laws on "racket abuse," apparently for Safin's benefit.) Certainly, he seemed to suggest, he could go through the motions, and earn his millions, but nothing about that process seemed to mean very much, at least in Palm Springs. It was, as all the players like to say, just a job, hard work.

"Games," suggested Christopher Lasch, "simultaneously satisfy the need for free fantasy and the search for gratuitous difficulty; they combine childlike exuberance with deliberately created complications. They re-create the remembered perfection of childhood, and mark it off from ordinary life with artificial boundaries."

The tennis played by Borg and McEnroe had sometimes looked a bit like that. For players like Safin, who had grown up knowing only these artificial boundaries and who carried that knowledge into their adult life, the possibility for childhood exuberance and remembered perfection seemed unlikely in the extreme. In making the sport entirely a business, in which children started their careers from birth, all recognisable sense of "play" had been forcibly removed from it. It seemed little wonder that the tennis authorities were concerned that the public did not connect emotionally with the game of

Safin's generation; the players hardly seemed to connect with it themselves.

If you have spent some part of almost every day of your life playing tennis then, I suppose, it is little surprise that you might become institutionalised. Serious tennis players often have superstitious respect for the lines that mark the court; often they won't step on them, like cracks in the pavement. They also come to view them, in some senses, as the boundary lines around their life.

In an interview Andre Agassi explained to me, in his gnomic way, how almost all of what went on in his head was about "the game inside the lines" and how, when you talk about tennis, "you are talking about a sport that transcends the lines of life. One on one, man to man. You are talking about how what I do affects what you do and how you deal with that. There's something *fundamental* there."

Given that much of their existence has been played out inside these lines, it is, you might imagine, a somewhat terrifying prospect for tennis players to imagine a life without them. For this reason, when considering his eventual retirement, Agassi sounded a little like Hamlet questioning his mortality. "Certainly I'm more afraid about how it is at the end right now, than what happens after," he said. "But as soon as I think about how it's going to end then I guess it's over. In thinking about the end the end is already there. What I hope," he said, "is that the fight happens in a way that I am proud of."

He had some good reasons for his anxiety about "the end," too. Few of the great players of the modern generation, those whose entire concentration has been channelled ruthlessly into the game, have been able to adjust to retirement with any ease.

Without the reassurance and discipline of the lines, Bjorn Borg's life, for example, once so ordered, quickly lost all shape and coherence as soon as he left them behind. Faced with all the messiness of life beyond tennis, the ascetic Borg appeared simply to go in search of the gratification he had always denied himself. He split from Simionescu within three years; had a relationship, and a child, with a seventeen-year-old whom he met when judging a wet T-shirt competition; and subsequently married, briefly, the Italian pop singer and soft-porn star Loredana Berte. His business ventures, centred round a range of clothing in which blouson jackets and lace-up pantaloons featured rather too heavily, left him nearly bankrupt. In 1989, only eight years after his last Wimbledon and still only thirty-three, he was rushed to hospital after overdosing on sleeping pills: ten hours a night was no longer enough. In subsequent years he found some kind of equilibrium, playing a little tennis on the Seniors Tour. But when I key in Borg's name to the search engine of my computer now the first reference it comes up with for the King of Wimbledon is a lingerie Web site.

Boris Becker's fall from grace on leaving the game was, if anything, even more dramatic. On the evening of his final match at Wimbledon, a straight sets loss to Pat Rafter, he recalled feeling more than usually estranged. His wife, Barbara Feltus, was seven months' pregnant with their second son and wanted him to spend the night at home with her, but Becker—the new Germany's model family man and idealist—wanted to go out, and "drink more and more with my buddies." He ended up at the West End restaurant Nobu where one of those "buddies," Angela Ermakova, a half-Russian, half-Algerian model, was waiting to induct him into the more complicated world of retirement. Suddenly, he later recalled, he was in a broom cupboard. "I had no idea what I was doing. It wasn't an affair. It was just *poom-bah-boom!*"

The first Feltus heard of this closet relationship was more than a year later, when she received a call from Ermakova herself, demanding $5 million from Boris to maintain the child that was the result of their brief union. Bizarrely, Becker alleged he had been the victim of a Mafia plot, that he'd enjoyed only oral sex with "that woman" and she had "stolen" his sperm. Eventually, after a DNA test, he admitted paternity. The first night of his retirement cost him, however, not only $3.5 million in maintenance payments, but also his marriage and a settlement to Feltus of $18 million; he then went straight from the divorce court to the state prosecutor's court, where he was given a suspended two-year prison sentence after admitting tax avoidance of more than $4 million.

To anyone who had followed John McEnroe's career it was hard to imagine that, on retirement, he would avoid this kind of fate. He cared about it too much and carried with him too many demons, it seemed, just to let it go. When his marriage to Tatum collapsed at the same time that his playing days were ending, some kind of spectacular fallout seemed inevitable.

Oddly, though, when he finally stepped away from the lines in 1993 McEnroe seemed not lost but liberated. There were clues in his final matches. His last Wimbledon ended as he might have hoped—with defeat in the semifinal by Agassi on Centre Court on July 4, and victory in the doubles with Michael Stich, 19–17 in the last set, the longest Wimbledon final ever. He won the Davis Cup with the help of Sampras and Agassi and, in the last tournament he ever won, in Chicago, he played his brother Patrick in the final. On that occasion, for the first time on court in a competitive match he managed something he had never felt able to express before: a joke. At match point a phone rang in the crowd. Despite who he was playing, despite the circumstances, part of McEnroe still wanted to explode. Another part of him, though, surprised himself. "Dad," he called out to his father in the stands, *"Mum's on the phone."*

For Christopher Lasch's Psychological Man, the usual defences against the traumas of ageing—which came so much earlier for sportsmen—were not available. Locked in the world of his own feelings, the narcissist, like a perpetual adolescent, was denied, Lasch suggested, "identification with ethical or artistic values beyond his immediate interests, intellectual curiosity, or the consoling warmth of relationships."

With McEnroe, though, it looked a little as if it had been the artificial confines of the game itself that had created his extremes of self-absorption all along. Now, off court and able to achieve a distance from its strictures, he seemed suddenly free to grow up.

One of the less successful outlets for his "intellectual curiosity" was his long-held ambition to become a rock star and, though he pursued this in earnest and took guitar lessons from Eric Clapton, he was able ultimately to take it less than seriously. I have tried, many times, to get hold of a recording of his Johnny Smyth Band but tragically, given the fact that McEnroe wrote the songs, too, none seems to exist. (One turning point in his musical career happened when David Bowie came to knock on his hotel room door to see if he fancied joining him for a drink, and then added the caveat "as long as you don't bring your guitar.")

Another more successful vehicle for McEnroe's restless attention was his art gallery. He had begun collecting paintings while he was playing—a huge silk screen Warhol had made of him had predictable pride of place in his Upper West Side apartment—and had visited galleries in many cities he went to on tour. When he retired he opened a gallery of his own, and for several years worked as an art dealer there pretty much full-time.

Initially, it was a way of escaping from the wreckage of his marriage. "I was really down and out at the time," he said in 1994. "I had just been separated and it was a godsend to be able to go to a place every day and keep my mind off what was going on." Soon, though, he had become fascinated by the work of several painters, particularly those whose emotional concerns seemed a match for his own.

Borg had once argued that "the chemistry of a tennis player is different from that of a painter. The artist is not judged as harshly. The artist does not win or lose every day in black and white terms as we do. Picasso did not have a 5–3 won/lost record with Van Gogh. But I have to live with my 5–3 record against McEnroe and try to see that the balance doesn't change."

Others were not so convinced of this distinction. Richard Evans, McEnroe's biographer, had described him as a "pointillist tennis player," likening his racket handling to Seurat's use of only the tip of his brush in painting. McEnroe himself saw the connections between art and tennis as rather more basic, however: "People in the art business have a tendency to one day tell you you're the greatest artist that ever lived and the next second make you wonder if you'll ever sell a piece of art again. So I think I have a knowledge of that, because you have a fear when you go on the court: fear of failure. . . . I understand [artists] are needy and insecure."

The artists he liked and bought were those who were able to translate some of this insecurity to canvas. They included Richard Diebenkorn and Alice Neel, but the painter McEnroe became closest to was Eric Fischl.

When you look at Fischl's work it seems to cast light on a similar set of preoccupations to those which possessed McEnroe on court, though admittedly somewhat obliquely: his most famous painting is of a sleepwalking teenage boy, bathed in Edward Hopper's American light, masturbating in a child's paddling pool. McEnroe appreciated the work, he said, "because of the very strong feelings about adolescence which he transfers to the canvas."

Fischl described how his paintings "from the beginning were generated by a lot of anger, focussed on the place I came from, the suburbs. . . . In the environment I grew up in there was no ability to acknowledge what the reality was. Everything was confined to a set of acceptable images, and they didn't conform to what was really happening." It seemed possible to argue that McEnroe had come up against a comparable sense of phoniness and "acceptable images" in tennis and beyond, at least in his own mind: the kind of thing, I suppose, I had seen in him when I had made my odd Salinger homage in 1983.

In response to these pressures, as the critic Robert Hughes observed, Fischl had "aspired to a way of drawing that was tense, dramatic and full of body." Dwelling on the latent frustrations of growing up, he wanted "an overall look that was not too finished, consistently 'imperfect' with an air of unconcern for its own mechanisms." This might be as good a description as any of McEnroe on court. Moreover, McEnroe appreciated, no doubt, that Fischl had found a way of always containing this frustration, his anger, between the lines, distancing himself from it a little, playing with it. In return, he taught the artist how to hit a backhand.

If his interest in art taught him something about adulthood, McEnroe had a chance to put that into practice in his second marriage, to the singer Patty Smyth, with whom he now has three children to add to the three he had with O'Neal, of whom he now has custody.

Bruno Bettelheim, the child psychologist who did his own growing up in Dachau and Buchenwald, defined the purpose of fairy tales as "assisting the growth process, which begins with a fear of growing up, and ends when youth has truly found itself, achieved psychological independence and moral maturity, and no longer views the other sex as frightening or demonic." McEnroe's own celebrity fairy tale, the fantasy marriage with his mirror image which ended in something of a Grimm's nightmare, seemed to have had just this kind of effect on him. The second time around he appears to have become more like the husband and father he always imagined he might be, before life within the lines got in the way.

When you see McEnroe play tennis on the Seniors Tour these days, he is introduced to the crowd as "the whole package: tennis player, art dealer, commentator, musician, husband, and father of six." He even allows himself a little smile at this, acknowledging that he is not yet a Renaissance man, still "a work in progress."

For the best part of a decade McEnroe has been in therapy, partly to deal with his "anger management issues," partly to appease Tatum's lawyers (in response, since he won custody of their three children, he has had Tatum take monthly dope tests). He feels that the therapy is helping a bit: "If I didn't think it helped, I wouldn't do it," he explained to me. "It's not as though I walk out of every session and think, God, I've made some advances, but when I look at the end of each year or six months I feel as though I'm heading in the right direction."

He is clear-eyed about his life on court. "I was like a compulsive gambler, or an alcoholic. Anger became a powerful habit. . . . The main reason I took a fair chunk of time off on two occasions was because that anger got out of control. Some part of me began to recognise that a human being should be in control of his emotions, and if I couldn't do that, I shouldn't be out there. . . . More and more I'm able to count to ten in situations that once would've gotten me going." (In the short-lived TV game show *The Chair*, McEnroe parodied his former self by trying to set contestants' pulses racing, monitoring their heartbeats while he asked quiz questions. After filming, one assistant producer observed some of these strategies: "Sometimes at the end of the day when he was really worked up John would go into the car park and get his tennis racket out and hit the air with it. I think it was a technique he used to control his anger.")

In holding on to this fragile peace with himself, by whatever means, he has also managed, triumphantly, to make peace with his old sparring partner, Wimbledon. As a commentator McEnroe brings everything that he always brought to his game—dexterity, timing, eloquence, controversy—but he adds an edge of distancing irony. Almost uniquely among those who talk about sport, it seems to me, he can respond in the here and now to what is happening on court. He makes it up as he goes along. "I never talk about what René Lacoste did in 1922," he says. "Nobody gives a rat's arse." For some people, those who want their rebel adolescents to stay rebel adolescents, he has, of course, sold out. David Foster Wallace, the author of the "great American novel" *Infinite Jest* and himself a former big-hitting junior tennis star, has argued that to "see McEnroe donning a blazer and doing truistic commentary is for me like seeing William

Faulkner do a Gap ad." Looked at another way, McEnroe has proved, far more gracefully than anyone might have expected, that, chalk dust or not, the lines are not the only thing after all. As a result, I'd say, he has achieved that very rare accomplishment, at least among celebrities: he has escaped his image, perhaps even his fate. In some ways, as a result, he may have allowed some of us to half-believe, at least for one fortnight a year, that we have grown up with him.

*Epilogue*

## Do Not Go Gently

Long after he had finished playing in the major leagues, the baseball legend Joe DiMaggio once turned out in an exhibition game in New York. In preparation, on the sidelines, he went through an elaborate ritual of practice and warm-up—so much so that before he stepped up to the plate a teammate, along for the appearance money, asked, "Joe, why do you still try so hard?" DiMaggio did not have to think too long about the question. "Well, you never know," he replied, "someone here might not have *seen me* before."

Watching McEnroe play in the Seniors events that he has dominated for the last four or five years, routinely beating men seven or eight years his junior, I'm reminded of DiMaggio's comment.

Out on court at the Albert Hall he is giving a full house a perfect impression of the man and the player he always was: creating every angle, arguing every call, staring at every line, making every volley, torturing himself over every missed ball. Even so, on this occasion his efforts don't prevent the umpire from making one announcement that you never expected to hear: "[Jeremy] Bates leads one set to love, McEnroe to serve . . ."

Despite his new, "mellow" adulthood, sitting in his chair beside the umpire, McEnroe seems unable quite to comprehend those words. On court, inside the lines, he is still the player he was. He is enquiring of the umpire when it was exactly that he last checked the height of the net. He is trading obscenities with the squiffy solicitors in Panama hats and braying bankers popping champagne corks up in the corporate boxes. He is kneeling as if in prayer to stretch some of the muscles in his long-suffering back. He is scratching his grey hair, slamming down his racket, slugging his Coke, still tying and untying his shoelaces, still stepping back onto court so slowly that every movement looks like it is achieved with unbearable mental effort, and still making the face that might cry at the indignity of it all. And then, of course, he starts to play a bit.

Without McEnroe there would be no Seniors Tour. It was Connors's idea to start with, but he did not carry on too long, of course, when McEnroe started beating him. There are other great players around, Grand Slam winners Becker, Cash, and Petr Korda, might-have-beens and should-have-beens like Guy Forget and Henri Leconte, never-quite-weres like Jeremy Bates and Mikael Pernfors, and all of them are in good shape, hitting the ball as well as ever, playing with a freedom, in some cases, that the pressures of the regular tour never allowed them. But McEnroe is the only one who can convince you that it's for real, the only one who can quiet the chink of cutlery on fine china from the hospitality crowd.

Afterwards, after he's beaten Bates quite easily in the end ("I was playing terribly, but I never really thought that I could ever, actually, like, *lose*"), I asked him if he ever wonders why he's still putting himself through all this.

He says no, there are never really any doubts for him. "Even today. I mean it was like I've got nothing to gain, but despite that kind of 'Why am I here?' malaise, in the midst of that, suddenly you find yourself in a really tough match with someone you should beat but who is playing some excellent tennis. And you've got to keep in your mind somewhere that this is not a bad deal all in all, that this is not a bad life, out here."

The other players, distanced in different ways from their games, tend to speak of him with a mixture of awe and wonder. There is something heroic, but almost comical, they say, when he gets on court, about how much he still cares. When you corner the likes of Cash and Forget, they find themselves giggling a little bit at "Johnny Mac's intensity." But they seem aware, too, that without McEnroe this kind of event would have no soul, would be just a circus, and that there's only so many times—once—you want to watch Henri Leconte handing the umpire his racket and taking over his chair, or the sideshow of paunchy Ilie Nastase, still showing off, playing shots between his legs. What the Senior Tour highlights dramatically is that tennis players, sports stars in general, are seldom amusing and never funny to order. Without McEnroe none of us would be here.

In some cases, it turns out, that is literally true. Petr Korda, only thirty-three and the Australian Open champion in 1998, has been persuaded to play at the Albert Hall against his will by the American. After he tested positive for nandrolene at Wimbledon in 1998, Korda, protesting his innocence, fell apart. One of the great natural (and mostly unfulfilled) talents, he lost his love for tennis entirely, did not pick up a racket at all for two years, and vowed never to do so again. This until McEnroe got on the phone to him.

"He kept calling me and asking me if I wanted to play the tour," Korda tells me, smiling thinly. "And my first thoughts were: No, no chance. I don't want to be part of anything. I wanted him to go away. But he kept on and eventually I went to see him play in Naples, and it was a really great crowd that night, he was playing Andres Gomez. And he tried everything on court to persuade me. He even did a scissor kick for me [this was the long-legged Korda's trademark gesture in victory] and pulled a muscle. After that I felt he wanted it so much, I couldn't say no, really, so I gave him my word to play six events."

McEnroe admits to attempting the same strong-arm tactics with other, younger players. He's forever, by his own admission, cajoling Jim Courier and Stefan Edberg to join the tour, and he talks like a teenager of how he can have his cake and eat it by being able to play both Korda and Becker in this tournament. (When he later hears that Becker has pulled out with a back injury, he sulks mightily.) "What I've been waiting for the last couple of years is what I'd call the final run of my career," he says, by way of explanation. "I've been watching and waiting for these guys specifically—Becker, Korda, and Edberg—to inspire me to see exactly what is left in my arsenal. But Becker is clearly someone incapable of any kind of consistency and I wonder if he'll be around at all. Edberg is hiding somewhere in Sweden. And Korda's gone through a lot of trials and tribulations these last few years."

He clearly despairs a little of this situation, cannot comprehend it. Typically, it's as if by refusing to appear, these players are deliberately ruining his own last throw of the dice. "If, say, Lendl wants to play celebrity golf, then that's his right and his decision, I suppose," McEnroe suggests, grudgingly. "I'm curious, though, when in conversations I've had with Edberg he tells me he's playing and practising on a regular basis, but then he won't come and get paid for it and play in front of people. I have no explanation for that. I can't see any reason for it."

The day after his victory over Bates, he is faced with the power of Korda's hitting, and you can see McEnroe's racket hand beginning to remember what it was once capable of: all the deftness of touch, the jabs and feints and angles begin to return. He loses narrowly, and graciously, but afterwards he is undoubtedly a little more alive.

"It's what I've been waiting for," he says, buzzing. "I mean it takes a bit of adjustment because the level was clearly so much higher. He was hitting shots that I don't normally see come back these days. Not many people have ever hit the ball as well as him. I probably wasn't as prepared as I should have been. But I know I'd like to play him again and I feel as though I can adapt and play better, take my level up." As he says this his face looks weary and grey, but his eyes are shining. "But I wanted to say now that I will not be playing tomorrow, my back hurts." He gets up to go, smiles. "Just kidding!" he says.

But the next day, against Guy Forget, McEnroe's

back is clearly hurting, and apparently his knees and his neck and his shoulders, wrists, and ankles are hurting, too. (This tournament, he says, "is for me a little like last man standing.") So, having seen the best of him, you now—anger management or not—get to see the rest.

Against the big-serving Forget he comes out snarling, raging against the dying of his light, the ways in which his body is letting him down, and this realisation is never really going to make McEnroe the player, say, philosophical.

Even so, the sheer force of his rage retains the power to shock. After every single failure to make a return on Forget's flashing serve, he holds his racket above his shoulder and considers the merits of smashing it. For no particular reason, early on, he demands to have a line judge replaced. And when the umpire does not take his request as seriously as he would like, he goes through a full repertoire of protest, the lines familiar, but still delivered entirely in earnest. "Why don't you just answer the question. I asked for him to be removed. Are you *going to do it?*" He calls for the referee, stages a long sit-down rant. He later rails nastily at the ball boys—"I don't want to spoil your system but I've only got two fucking balls"—and at the end of a game in which he is broken he kicks the little Ellesse box that surrounds another line judge, a prim woman in her fifties, and says, only half to himself, "fucking asshole." The woman paces around to the umpire to report him and then walks slowly back past McEnroe, with him scowling at her all the way. After the next point he does exactly the same thing—the kick, the comment. And then he asks the woman, like a schoolboy: "What are you waiting for? Go tell him, see what happens."

In between his rages, on court, he squanders ten set points, mostly to Forget's aces, and towards the end he's lying on his back at changeovers trying to coax some life into his knackered muscles, spitting fury at anyone who crosses his eyeline. Every time the umpire calls time, McEnroe looks as if he's been reminded of his mortality.

While he is lying flat out like this, as, more than twenty years ago, he lay flat out at the end of his Wimbledon defeat to Borg, someone who does not understand yells out to him from the expensive seats, "Come on, Mac, it's only the Seniors." For a moment you can see him thinking about it, but in the end McEnroe doesn't even bother to begin to explain that he's doing it all for love.

**ABOUT THE AUTHOR**

*TIM ADAMS has been an editor at* Granta *and* Literary Editor *of* The Observer, *where he now writes full-time. He lives in London with his wife and two daughters.*